A PASTOR'S SECRETS

A PASTOR'S SECRETS

FOR YOUNG PASTORS...AND THOSE WANTING TO BE A PASTOR

RONNIE MEEK

WordCrafts Press

A Pastor's Secrets
Copyright © 2023
Ronnie Meek

ISBN: 978-1-957344-82-9

Cover concept and design by Jonathan Grisham for Grisham Designs

Published by WordCrafts Press
Cody, Wyoming 82414
www.wordcrafts.net

Contents

To Harvey and Margaret Meek
my long suffering parents
who showed me what it means to be faithful.

PREFACE

This is not a "How To" book. This is a book of things I have experienced and observed and learned over forty years of full time ministry.

The reason I wrote this book is because after decades of interacting with other Pastors it is pretty clear that I tend to see things through a somewhat unconventional lens. I don't claim to be *right* about everything, but I do know that it can often be helpful to see things from a different angle. We all tend to get stuck in our own assumptions. We take our infinite God and try to make Him work within our distinctly finite perspectives. My prayer is that this book will help in some small way to knock off some of the crust that may have formed around our eyes as we endeavor to lead His flock.

My father was a Pastor. My maternal grandfather was a Pastor. I grew up around Pastors and Evangelists and Missionaries. I became a Youth Pastor at age 32, was on the Mission field in Zimbabwe for three years from age 35 to 38, and until retirement this past year I Pastored a single church from age 38 to 71. I don't claim to know everything, but over the years I have observed a few things about being a Pastor, and this book is my humble contribution to the subject.

PART 1
BECOMING A PASTOR

WHAT IS A PASTOR?

There were just over 140 in my high school class. Three of us became Pastors. Hank was not one of the three, but he knew all three quite well and was one of my best friends in high school. As is often the case, life took us in dissimilar directions, and shortly after graduation we lost touch for several decades. We reconnected in our sixties. One day at lunch Hank made an observation which he seemed to find somewhat novel. He stated that it seemed that as a Pastor I did not consider my primary duty to be a bringer of the gospel, but rather one who sought to bring spiritual growth and unity to the church I had led for almost thirty-three years. He was right, and I was flattered.

Most people in the American Protestant church seem to believe that the terms "Preacher" and "Pastor" are interchangeable. They are not. A Pastor may very well be a Preacher, but that only defines a small portion of his or her duties. Ephesians 4:11 denotes five different leadership callings in the Church: Apostle, Prophet, Evangelist, Pastor, and Teacher. All of these callings can involve preaching. A Pastor is in fact called to be a Shepherd. To define a Pastor as simply a Preacher is like defining a shepherd as someone whose only job is to talk to sheep.

This unfortunate pairing of the terms Pastor and Preacher has created some challenging side effects for the Church. Perhaps the most damaging side effect has been to cause those who have a charismatic personality or a gift for communicating to often be positioned as Pastors when they are just as often ill-suited for such a calling.

When Samuel went to the house of Jesse to anoint one of Jesse's sons to be king over Israel, the first son presented to him was Eliab, the eldest. Eliab looked so much like a king that even Samuel was tempted to anoint him straight away. Samuel thought, Surely the *LORD's anointed stands here before the LORD*. He was wrong. Fortunately Samuel was in the habit of listening to the Lord. The Lord said to Samuel, "Do not consider his appearance or his height, for I have rejected him. The LORD does not look at the things people look at. People look at the outward appearance, but the LORD looks at the heart."

People look at the outward appearance, and as a result many churches are being *Pastored* by an Eliab. Actually, they are being led, but they are not being Pastored at all. Eliab is neither called nor capable to be a Pastor even though he certainly looks the role. He may be well suited to lead a Fortune 500 company. He may in fact be a great preacher, but when it comes to fulfilling the actual role of a true Pastor he is unfortunately lacking.

I used to hold a monthly Saturday morning meeting with some of the young men who seemed to be rising leaders in our church. There was one young man in particular whom I was considering as a candidate to some day take my place as the Senior Pastor. This young man had only been a believer around five years, but he had already exhibited a willingness to seriously study the Scriptures. He was already an above average teacher. Furthermore, he had a kind of charisma that drew people to him. He had many good qualities including what seemed to be a healthy dose of genuine humility. He was rising up my list until one meeting when he made the comment, "If the boat is sinking I'm going to be the first one off." The young man was already a good preacher, but he was not ever going to be Pastoral material unless he could get to the place where if the boat were sinking he would see to it that everyone else was off before himself.

When Hank made his comment about me seeming to consider my role as a Pastor to be less a bringer of the gospel and more concerned with leading our congregation, I replied, "My calling as a Christian is to bring the gospel. My calling as a Pastor is to prepare others to follow Christ." Bringing the gospel is only the first step in following Christ. For a Pastor to simply bring the gospel and consider their job done is like one who gives birth and thinks there is nothing more to being a parent. Actually, the job has just started.

THE CALL

Jesus told His disciples, "You did not choose me. I chose you."
A person cannot just decide to be a Pastor. One must be called.
Unfortunately, there are organizations that will declare a person to
be a Pastor based on fulfilling educational requirements or other
such criteria that have nothing to do with being called by God.
This does a great disservice to the Kingdom of God, but it often
does help support the organization's coffers. (If I seem a bit cynical
at times please understand that I am seventy-two years old. I don't
mean to be bad spirited, but I do tend to call things as I see them.)

How does one know if they are called?

There is no set formula concerning how one is called. Some people
can point to a specific moment or event. One friend of mine sat
up in bed in the middle of the night and simply announced to
his wife, "I've been called to be a Pastor!" He recently retired after
over forty years of fruitful ministry.

You might think that being the son—and grandson—of a Pastor
had something to do with my call. Perhaps it did but not in the
way you would think. I grew up in a church of about 120 where
everyone knew everyone else. Being the son of the Pastor (I was also

an only child), and having some communication gifts, it seemed that everyone assumed I would become a Pastor. However, being a contrarian and seeing the things a Pastor and his family had to deal with, the last thing I ever wanted to be was a Pastor. I spent my late teen years through my mid-twenties as a prodigal wanting nothing to do with the Church. When I finally surrendered to the Lord and returned to the fold it was not with an awareness of a call to Pastor. Had that been part of the deal, I'm not at all sure I would have come back.

For me the call was not so dramatic as my friend mentioned above. I simply had a quiet assurance that I had been called and that God would open the right door at the right time. Some six years later I was called into the office of the outgoing Youth Pastor at our church and asked if I would be interested in taking the job. I said, "Yes." Somewhat taken aback by my prompt response I was asked, "Don't you want to pray about it?" I replied, "I don't need to. I know this is what I'm supposed to do."

How does one know if they have been called is not a question that can be answered by saying "thus and such will happen;" however, it is a question that can be answered quite simply. If you are not certain that you have been called, then you haven't been called—at least not yet. The individual is the only one who can truly know if they have been called because the call to be a Pastor is a uniquely personal matter between an individual and his or her God. If one does not have that kind of relationship with God then it is safe to say they are not called to shepherd His flock.

Moses had a burning bush experience, but I suspect that is more of an outlier than the norm. I believe the norm would be more in line with Peter, Andrew, James, and John. We read about Jesus coming to them while they were fishing—plying their trade—and saying, "Follow me." They immediately left their former trade and started following Jesus. It seems so dramatic, but the reality was likely much less so. They already knew Jesus. They had been close with John the Baptist. The decision to leave their nets and follow

Christ was not a spur of the moment impulse. It was already their desire to leave and follow Jesus. So, when He gave the invitation they were ready.

"Would you like to be the next Youth Pastor?"

"Yes."

How does one prepare for the ministry?

For many people in our culture the call to Pastor is automatically connected to attending a seminary. So it was, about two years after I came back to the Lord, I applied to attend a nearby seminary. While my college years had been spent running from the Lord, they had not been spent running to class. I was less than a stellar student, but I did graduate and had a GPA in the low 3s. Apparently that wasn't good enough for seminary. I received a rejection letter. I wasn't discouraged. This wasn't a sign that I wasn't called. This simply meant that this wasn't the path God had for me.

I believe seminary has an important role to play in the Kingdom of God; however, I'm not sure that role is best served in the training of Pastors. I am thankful for the role seminaries play in training people for the work of the study of ancient languages, counseling, and certain areas of teaching, but these are only tangentially connected to the work of a Pastor. After one's relationship to the Lord, the primary concern of a Pastor is the flock one is called to lead. Sometimes these other areas can become such a focus in one's life that the flock is relegated to secondary importance. During my years on the mission field I earned a seminary degree online, and I have several Pastor friends who have seminary degrees. Without exception we would all say that our undergraduate degree as been more useful in the actual execution of our duties as a Pastor.

There are other ways one can prepare for the work of a Pastor. In my case it was personal experience coupled with consistent daily study of the Bible over a period of years. Before becoming a Pastor, I served in several volunteer capacities. I sang in the choir.

I changed the outdoor church sign weekly. I taught junior high Sunday school. (There is a special place in heaven for those who have taught junior high Sunday school.) I worked in the nursery. I led worship. I was a youth worker, and I served as an Elders. Before becoming a Senior Pastor I spent two and a half years as a Youth Pastor and three years as a Missionary in Zimbabwe teaching in a Bible school. By the time I became a Senior Pastor (initially the church was small enough that I was the only Pastor) I had quite a bit of first-hand knowledge about many of the positions needed in a healthy local fellowship. While serving in these other capacities I was not consciously aware of being prepared to lead as a Senior Pastor, but in retrospect that was excellent training for what lay ahead.

Why would someone uncalled be attracted to the ministry?

From the vantage of an outside onlooker being a Pastor can appear to be quite attractive. As long as one isn't afraid of public speaking, the job seems to be easy. One or two days a week you work for a few hours and the rest of the time you retreat to your study to talk to God, read books, and relax. There is also the high level of respect accorded to Pastors and all that free time you have to fish or play golf. Of course the reality is far different.

Pastors are truly on call 24/7. When our church hired an Assistant Pastor we initially created this as a part-time position. The lady we brought on to fill the position had grown up as a PK (Preacher's Kid). We were only offering a part-time salary. The first thing I said to her was, "You know there is no such thing as a part-time Pastor, just a part-time salary." She knew. My own father was always bi-vocational, but just because he worked another full time job to put food on the table did not mean that he wasn't a full-time Pastor as well.

The reality behind the curtain is that for most Pastors sharing the Word and preparing to share the Word are the easiest parts of the job. The rest of the story involves dealing with people. It doesn't take long to discover that just because people come to church doesn't mean they actually hear the sermons, or even the announcements. Furthermore, people have opinions. They have opinions about theology, about service structure, about your wife's dress, about your kids' behavior, about the car you drive, about how much you should be paid, and a great many other things. Often these opinions are ill informed and frequently none of their business, but you must still love them and try to lead them. Most difficult of all is that many have an opinion about how you should do your job.

There was an occasion when I had to let a Youth Pastor go. Actually, over my thirty-plus years at our church there were three such occasions, but following this particular one I had a couple with a long standing attachment to the church come to me to inform me that I had made a mistake. They had heard from the Lord, and I must bring this Youth Pastor back on staff. I explained that the reason I had let this particular person go was because I felt that I had heard from the Lord, and while I respected them and their opinion I couldn't make a decision—the results of which were my responsibility—based on what they advised instead of what I felt the Lord was saying to me. They left the church.

Probably the hardest thing to deal with as a Pastor is when those who are influential in the church disagree with something you are doing and take their opinion privately public. Privately public simply means that they are not openly opposing you, they are just talking with a few people and perhaps soliciting prayer. This is particularly challenging when they are someone you consider to be a close friend.

Does this actually happen?

Do people eat food and breathe air?

Why is the "Call" necessary?

Being a Pastor is hard. It is hard in terms of the hours worked. I did not require regular office hours from myself or my staff. My reasoning was that the people weren't at our offices, and it was more important for us to be among the people. We may not have always been in the office from eight-to-five, but we were always available. In our secular American culture it seems to be a sin to be *idle*. Many Pastors feel pressure to always be doing something to prove they really are working. They put in a *full day at the office* only to leave the office and discover that this is often when the real job starts. The result is burnout, burnout, and more burnout. When they are called on outside the office hours, it doesn't take long for people to become a nuisance rather than the actual work of the Pastor. There is simply no time to be still, even though the Bible commands, "Be still and know that I am God."

Being a Pastor is often hard financially. It is easy to get distracted by the high flying life style of the Celebrity Pastor, but that is so wrong on so many levels. The reality is that the majority of Pastors need an outside job to support their family. There are those who are able to support a family on a Pastor's salary but that usually requires years of careful budgeting. This is not a complaint. God is faithful and it is a great blessing to be able to trust in His provision, but for all Pastors this truth has to pass from mere words to on the ground experience. Not everyone has that kind of faith. The person with great faith isn't the one with the private jet but the one with the second hand car who is continuing to faithfully serve.

Being a Pastor is hard emotionally. People will let you down. There will be seasons when it seems that you are a failure. People are complaining. The church isn't *growing*. No one seems to be listening to your sermons. The temptation to compare yourself to the Pastor on the billboard or on the book jacket is so strong. Even worse, the desire to *be* the Pastor on the billboard or the book jacket bubbles up inside you. All of those uninformed ideas about how respected you would be as a Pastor lie crumpled at the base of a concrete wall of reality. Isolation sets in. Perhaps even depression.

So, if being a Pastor is so hard why continue to do it? The Call.

I was greatly blessed during my years in full time ministry to be able to support my family without having to do full time outside work. I was greatly blessed to have a clear awareness of the dangers and signs of burnout. I was greatly blessed to always have genuine friends and so avoid isolation. I was greatly blessed to have a wife who understood the pressures of ministry and was always supportive. (Being a Pastor's wife is itself a calling.) I could go on, but suffice it to say I understand that I had it pretty easy. There were no church splits and no attempts to remove me from my job. Nevertheless, I had numerous occasions when I sincerely called out to the Lord, "Please! Let me do anything but this." It is the Elijah Syndrome. Even after his greatest service where he called fire down from heaven, a few days later Elijah was crying, "Take me home, Lord. I'm worthless here."

If you go into the ministry as a Pastor this will happen. The only reason you will stay at your post is the Call. If you know that you know that you have been called by God, what are you going to say, "No?"

THE ANOINTING

T here is much truth in the notion that God doesn't call those who are able to do the task; rather, He enables those He calls to do the task. There is a specific term for this enablement when it comes to serving God in an area of ministry. That term is "the anointing."

What is *the anointing*?

The best description I have ever heard of the anointing was spoken by Ezekiel Guti while I was teaching Bible school in Zimbabwe. Ezekiel Guti was the founder of the school where I was teaching, and one day he arrived to speak to the students and staff at the chapel service. He had many leaders under his oversight in the ministry, and several of these leaders were designated as Evangelists. One Evangelist in particular was quite successful. His name was Abel Sandy.

Brother Guti was talking about the anointing and stated that Abel Sandy was an anointed Evangelist. He went on to explain how he knew this, and the explanation was so clear and powerful that it still resonates with me decades later. He said that one of us could preach a powerful message of salvation and issue an invasion to accept Christ only to see a few people respond and come forward. Sandy could speak to the same crowd for five minutes then simply hold out his arms and say, "Come to Jesus." The result would be that almost every unsaved person in the crowd would come running forward. That is the anointing.

If you are going to have a fruitful ministry, the anointing is necessary, because it is impossible for you to *do* anything for God on your own. Jesus said in John 15:5 "Apart from me you can do nothing." He told Nicodemus in John 3:6, "Flesh gives birth to flesh, but Spirit gives birth to spirit." You can draw a crowd without the anointing. You can build an impressive organization without the anointing. You can create a successful brand in the world's eyes without the anointing. You can sell a lot of books and have a lot of followers on social media without the anointing. Frankly, you can even *prophesy* and do great miracles without the anointing. (See Matthew 7:22) However, you cannot bear any fruit that will last in the Kingdom of God without the anointing.

How does one come to receive *the anointing*?

It is certainly not wrong to want to receive God's anointing; however, it is most certainly wrong to seek God's anointing with wrong motives. Some people may desire to receive the anointing simply out of a desire to be recognized as one of those who are anointed. During my years as a Pastor I've had numerous occasions where people have unformed me that they are a prophet. I can honestly say that considering all of the ones who have felt it necessary to enlighten me regarding their *anointing*, I have yet to hear a truthful prophetic word from any of them.

We live in a broken world filled with broken people. So many feel the need to standout in some way in order to feel their worth. That is the wisdom of the world, and it leads to nothingness. What so many fail to understand is that our worth is not connected to what we do so much as it is a function of who we are. We are, each of us, of inestimable worth because Jesus gave His life for us. There is nothing I can do that can ever add anything to value such as that.

We see instances in Scripture of people coming to Jesus wanting to be His disciple. When this happens Jesus doesn't tell them "no," he simply tells them what is required, and then we never hear about them again. In the case of the Twelve He comes and calls them. (There is the situation in John's Gospel where Andrew and another of John's disciples come to Jesus, but they are sent by John the Baptist, and they simply ask Jesus where He is staying.) Therefore, we hear Jesus saying to the Twelve, "You did not choose me, but I chose you and appointed you so that you might go and bear fruit—fruit that will last." John 15:16 (NIV)

A case can be made for saying the anointing comes by the laying on of hands or some other such ritual. However, the basic truth is that the anointing is not something that comes by the will of any man. God is the one who choses, and only He can truly anoint. He will often pass over the obvious choice, such as the impressive older brother, and select the forgotten younger brother. He may often choose the reluctant, such as Moses or Gideon—the fact remains that He alone chooses.

There can be value in having someone farther along in the faith recognize a gifting in your life. I was ordained by the Assemblies of God in a meaningful ceremony after completing a period of testing and exams. Other groups have even more extensive periods and methods of examination before ordaining a candidate for ministry. Some go so far as to claim an unbroken connection to the initial Apostles—the idea being that Jesus had the authority to bestow the call (which he certainly did) and that He passed such authority on to those Apostles who then passed it on to certain others who again passed it on down through the ages until it finally rest upon the person now being ordained. The issue isn't whether Jesus had such authority, or even whether the early Church leaders had such authority, but whether after Jesus they alone had the authority to pass it on and whether those to whom it was passed over the years

15

have always continued to move under the direction of the Holy Spirit or if they strayed to other motives.

It can be powerful and meaningful to have the laying on of human hands confirm one's call to the ministry; however, it is possible to pass the needed requirements and receive such a human *anointing* without a true call from God. In such a case the bestowed anointing is only of man's origin and is no true anointing from God.

Some people would say the anointing comes from seeking to receive it directly from the Holy Spirit. Clearly receiving an anointing from the Holy Spirit is from God and has great value; however, there is very little *clear* about how to know if someone has indeed received an anointing from the Holy Spirit. Even signs and wonders can deceive and are not clear evidence. Furthermore, there is scant instruction in Scripture regarding the idea that we should seek something that is so clearly the prerogative of God's sovereignty.

Additionally, we need to understand that not all anointings are permanent in nature. Paul instructs all believers to desire to prophesy. All believers can prophesy, but that does not mean that all believers are prophets. God can anoint any believer to bestow the grace of supernatural healing, but that does not mean that such a person has now become a *healer*.

There are cases where the anointing is permanent, or at least it is meant to be. Saul was anointed to be king by God's sovereign will, but because of his willful disobedience that anointing was lost. David was also anointed to the same calling. David was not perfect, but he recognized that without the anointing he was nothing, and so he would pray, "Do not take your Holy Spirit from me."

The anointing to be a Pastor is of an ongoing permanent nature. It is an anointing to run a marathon, not a sprint. It is not proved by the number of names on the church roll, the volume of book sales, impressive billboard sightings, or any other worldly metric. It is proved over the years by the faithful exercise of the Pastoral calling to shepherd the people of God. In many ways it is the most humble of all ministry callings which also means that from a Kingdom perspective it is likely also the greatest.

How does one receive such an anointing? As with receiving the Call, I can only say that it is a highly personalized matter. Some may have a burning bush experience. Some may have a Samuel announce the anointing or an Elijah throw his cloak over them. Some may simply place their hand to the plow and not look back. In every case one thing holds true. A person can only receive that which is given to them from above.

One important point about the Pastoral Anointing

Just because you have been anointed to be a Pastor does not mean that you also carry other anointings in your ministry.

I grew up in a small church that never grew beyond twenty-five or thirty families. When I took my position as the Pastor of the church in Smyrna, Tennessee, we had perhaps fifty people total in the church. In such situations the Pastor is often expected to do everything. This may involve cutting the grass and cleaning the toilets. Such tasks can be easily done. The real problem of the *do-everything* Pastor comes in the realm of spiritual activities. As a Pastor you teach (preach) and visit those who are sick or shut in. You perform weddings and funerals. You meet with those who need spiritual guidance. All of these things are simply part of the job description; however, there are often other expectations to which you are not called and for which you are not anointed.

One of the things that seemed to come with the job in the tradition I grew up with was that the Pastor should also be a powerful intercessor. I'm quite sure that there are a good many Pastors who have an intense prayer life where they spend hours at a time travailing before the Throne for those in need. I'm not one of those Pastors. I am certainly not making light of those who function that way. I am simply saying that is not who God created me to be. God created me to be the kind of person whose prayer life is more of a running dialogue than hours in the *prayer closet*. The *prayer warrior* type tends to carry a pretty heavy load and seems to often have a *burden* for matters that can only be relieved by long periods of travail. That would crush me. God made me to travel light with the result that during decades of full time ministry whenever I would hear, "Pastor will you pray for…" I would stop and say, "Let's pray right now." I have seen many prayers answered and managed to not be crushed nor be particularly impressed with myself.

The point is to know who you are and who God has called you to be. Not every Pastor is the same. Some are great speakers while some are great listeners. Some are pioneers while others are equipped with gifts of administration. The pioneer will likely struggle greatly to lead a large congregation while the gifted administrator will give up and quit the start-up after a few months (or years) of fifty one week and six the next week. Just because you are a Pastor does not mean that God called you to be someone other than who you are. If you are a great listener, it is unlikely that God has anointed you to be the guy with the big television ministry. He can use you in this way if He so chooses, but just because He uses another Pastor that way doesn't mean that is how He wants to use you.

It is vitally important that you walk in your unique calling as a Pastor because your primary task is to shepherd the callings and gifting of others. I was not a heavy-lifter intercessor, and I did not try to be. (Actually, I did try to be but soon discovered I was like a cello in a marching band.) Once I realized an area for which I did not have an anointing, I would start asking God to fill that need, and He would send others who were so anointed. If I did not acknowledge such a deficiency in myself these others could not have fulfilled their calling because I would be in the way. Worse, I might have resented their gifting and like Saul with David rejected some of the greatest gifts God was sending to the ministry. God equips those He calls, but as a Pastor you must realize that part of that equipping involves those He sends you rather than the gifts you have yourself.

PART 2

BEING A PASTOR

Focus on Christ

Our church held a retirement service for me. Several dear friends in the ministry came, and each said a few words. Each one meant a great deal to me and was greatly appreciated. The last to speak was Fr. Ray Kasch. Ray is an Anglican Rector, and we have both Pastored in the same town for over twenty years. We have spoken to each other's congregations and shared many hours in rich fellowship over the years. I believe we know each other pretty well. When Ray spoke at my retirement service, he said that most long term Pastors have a main theme to their ministries. He said that my theme had been simply to exalt Christ. I was deeply moved, because that is my theme, and I was humbled that apparently it had been noticed.

It would seem that this point of focus would be so obvious that it would hardly need to be mentioned; however, in actual practice I find this is often not the case. While I believe that virtually all churches would say Christ is their focus, the reality is often quite different. So, what are some things that tend to displace Christ as the focus of a church?

Doctrine

I grew up in the Assemblies of God but left the Faith entirely from my late teens till my mid-twenties. I came back to the Faith in my mid-twenties and in my early thirties I entered full time ministry in a non-denominational setting. In my late thirties I agreed to become the Pastor of the church where my dad had been Pastoring. My dad was seventy-two and ready to retire. This particular church was in the Assemblies of God. I guess what goes around often does come around.

In order to Pastor this church I was going to need to be ordained by the Assemblies of God, so my dad took me to meet with the District Superintendent. The DS was a man I had known since childhood, and we had a very pleasant meeting and conversation. Finally we got around to the topic of me being ordained, and the DS asked me, "Are there any doctrinal issues that might be a problem for you being in the Assemblies?" I gave a sheepish smile and said, "I don't believe I'm going to be able to teach that unless one has spoken in tongues they have never been filled with the Holy Spirit." He paused and finally said, "Of course you know you've touched on one of the pillars." I did know that, but what are you going to do?

We talked around things for awhile. This church I was agreeing to lead needed a Pastor, and the DS apparently thought I'd make a worthwhile Pastor in spite of my position about one of *the pillars*. I finally agreed with his proposition that, while a supernatural physical manifestation might not be the most important or convincing evidence of the infilling of the Holy Spirit—and might not even be supernatural at all being fairly easy to fake—if one were to look for a supernatural physical evidence of the infilling of the Holy Spirit, then speaking in tongues would be the most likely biblical candidate. If that last sentence seems a bit convoluted to you, I feel your pain. The conclusion was that I was welcomed to the fellowship and ordained.

The Assemblies of God refers to the teaching that only those who have experienced speaking in tongues can truly be said to be filled with the Holy Spirit as our Pentecostal Distinctive. Speaking in tongues is known as the initial physical evidence (IPE). I doubt that there is an Assemblies of God church anywhere that would not claim that Christ is their essential and most important focus; however, there are plenty who would be quick to expel from the fellowship any who don't hold fast to the doctrine of the IPE.

Full disclosure, I have a great deal of love and respect for the Assemblies of God; however, after twenty-two years as an ordained Assemblies of God Pastor, I resigned in good standing, and our church became a non-denominational fellowship.

The Assemblies of God is by no means the only group that places great emphasis on what I would consider to be a non-essential doctrine. I would not even consider the Assemblies to be one of the more extreme in this regard. Several years ago there was a young man who came to our town to start a Lutheran Church (Wisconsin Synod). I invited him to share lunch with several of the Pastors in town. We were having what seemed to be a nice time of fellowship until the food came. I asked this young man if he would say a blessing over the food, and he declined. One of the other Pastors volunteered, and we all started to join hands when this same brother declined to join hands. We asked him why, and he stated that unless he knew where we all stood on doctrine he could not be sure we were Christians. True story.

There are many who would claim that their main focus is to exalt Christ, yet they cluster into camps bringing division to the Body of Christ for the sake of non-essential and (I'm just going to say it) often petty doctrines. These may concern baptisms, or eschatology (end times teaching), or styles of worship, or biblical translations, etc., etc., etc. Please!

Believe what you want to believe about such things. We are all just seeing through a glass darkly anyway. But these things are not what we are called to focus on as Pastors or as Christians. We are called to lift up Christ and not some doctrinal position, much less a particular organization. Sometimes it isn't even doctrine getting in the way. Sometimes it is culture.

Culture

We are all greatly shaped by our culture. In the West we think of
Eastern culture, African culture, Middle Eastern culture, Tribal
culture, Island culture, etc., as being strange. Perhaps we find it
to be beautiful, but we might just as easily find it repulsive and
wonder, "How can anyone live like that?" What we fail to understand is that these cultures look at us and think the same things.
The Netflix show *The Crown* has a scene where Margaret Thatcher
is complaining to the Queen about the British Commonwealth.
Mrs. Thatcher believes that Briton is superior to all these other
nations with their tribal leaders wearing costumes. The Queen
replies, "Is that not what I am? A tribal leader wearing costumes?"

Culture blinds us to so much. It does not blind God, because
He created and fully understands them all. The Bible tells us that
around His throne is a great multitude wearing white robes. These
are people from every nation, tribe, people, and language. Though
they are from such different cultures, they are all saying the same
thing: "Salvation belongs to our God who sits on the throne, and
to the Lamb." In other words, it is Christ, not culture, that unifies
us and qualifies us to stand in the presence of God.

Part of the genius of the Gospel is that it is not tied to a particular culture. Hinduism is tied to a culture. Islam is largely tied
to a culture. Judaism (in its orthodox form) is tied to a culture.
Many other beliefs and cults are easily identifiable by their culture.
Christianity is not tied to any particular culture. It is simply tied to
faith in Christ. Yet, in the American Church we often find culture
to be preached as much, or even more than, Christ. I would suggest
that Christ is often relegated to a prop to support our particular
ideas about culture.

There is a long history of people in the church requiring certain modes of dress. They take a passage like 1 Timothy 2:9–10;
*I also want the women to dress modestly, with decency and propriety,
adorning themselves, not with elaborate hairstyles or gold or pearls or*

expensive clothes, but with good deeds, appropriate for women who profess to worship God. (NIV) to support their ideas about what is *godly.* There is nothing wrong with this passage except, who gets to decide what is modest and decent? Those are pretty broad terms. Is it OK to wear a gold wedding band? In our culture that's a pretty important and decent accessory. Furthermore, Paul doesn't even say this is from the Lord. He says, "This is what I want." Nevertheless, a passage such as this one is taken and becomes the focus of what we preach and do and expect and argue about in the church. Where is Christ?

It is actually worse than this. In 1979 there was an organization called The Moral Majority formed by Pastor Jerry Falwell Sr. Its goal was to influence politicks to adopt laws and policies that it perceived to be godly and take back the culture for God. The results have been pretty clear in terms of our culture, but not what Pastor Falwell envisioned. I don't think anyone would argue that we have a more godly culture now than we did forty years ago. However, in terms of its impact on the church it has been an unmitigated disaster. The statistics are clear. Church attendance in the late 1970s was around 70%. Today it is around 47%. Today almost 65% of people in the USA identify as Christian. That sounds good but in 1980 that figure was 89%.

Instead of repenting for placing Christ in the corner, we find more and more churches doubling down on the *Culture Wars.* When we preach and argue about politicks and culture, we go down a rabbit hole from which few ever return. Everyone has an opinion, and the arguments can be endless. When we focus on Christ all of that is eliminated. There is no argument. Christ is beautiful. He did not say, "If you will fight for your idea of righteousness I'll draw all men to it." He said, "If I am lifted up I will draw all men to myself."

When in the pulpit, I eventually learned to avoid any mention of politicks or divisive cultural issues. The main reason was that Jesus and the Apostles never go there. If you really want old time religion, you can't get there with culture preaching. Another reason I don't address these things is because they are inevitably divisive. Once you release that spirit of division in the church it is like trying to ski uphill to keep division from spreading into every crack and crevice of the fabric of the fellowship. Finally, the reason why I don't mention it is because once you push one of these hot buttons you've lost the people. You may only spend two minutes of a thirty minute sermon on one of these hot button issues, but those two minutes will be the topic of 98% of any discussion that follows.

We are not called to use the current hot issue to get more page views. We are not called to gather followers around the latest conspiracy theory, or nationalism, or whatever it is that the culture focuses on. We need to repent of the sin of creating all of this useless noise. We are called to exalt Christ.

Personal Advancement

In 1975 I left my prodigal way and came home to the Lord. I was ravenously hungry. Any night of the week when there was a service or a Bible Study to attend, I was there. I remember one night in particular going with some friends to a small church in East Nashville to hear a speaker they were excited about. I don't remember the speaker's name, and I don't remember much about the sermon, except I clearly remember the main point of the sermon. The main point concerned a story about his son who now traveled with them and played drums for the ministry. It seems that somehow or another the son had believed in faith, and the Lord had given him a (wait for it) Lincoln automobile! But there was more. Through faith the Lord had also given the speaker a Lincoln automobile! The point of the sermon was that if you have faith then you too could receive a Lincoln automobile. The opportunity to express your faith was soon presented by the passing of the offering plate.

We were in a church. We sang the kind of songs you sing in a church. We heard a speaker who occasionally referenced the Bible, just like in a church, but something just didn't feel right. Before I reached home that night it hit me; I left the service thinking about Lincoln automobiles instead of Jesus. The thought has stuck with me ever since that if you go to a *service* and Jesus has taken a backseat to something else, then something is wrong.

Politicks and the Culture Wars are not the only reasons for the decline of the Church in the USA. In 1952 Dr. Norman Vincent Peale wrote a book called *The Power of Positive Thinking*. The book was sort of a self-help guide to using visualization techniques along with some biblical underpinnings to develop an optimistic attitude. It was not well received by health experts, theologians, and scholars, but of course that has never stopped the American public. It became quite popular and influential. There was not so much wrong with it as long as you didn't take it too far. However, or culture is noted for taking things too far.

Within a couple of decades teachings were rising in the church about using these very techniques to get what you want. The claim was that if you could visualize it and believe it enough (also called exercising your faith) then God was supposedly bound by His Word to give it to you. Proof texts were trotted out and any balancing texts were ignored. The hyper faith *name-it and claim-it and have-it* theology was born.

Were any results produced?

Yes.

Some people developed a better attitude and probably a better life experience. Many people tried, but apparently their faith just couldn't cut it. As a result they became at best disillusioned with the Church and often embittered and broken. (As Cousin Eddie says, "If only I had that money Catherine and I gave to that TV Preacher who was screwin' that hockey player.") But there were two other results that have continued to echo and amplify over the intervening decades. One result was the emergence of the Celebrity Pastor flush with cash and a high flying life style. There have always been those who were only in it for the money, but hyper faith along with TV and book sales have made that enterprise more alluring than ever. The other result was the widespread relegation of Christ to a fund raising prop, if He was even mentioned at all.

Instead of lifting up Christ, the *Church* was now lifting up prosperity and success. The goal was no longer to receive Christ and humbly take up your cross and follow Him. The goal was now to exercise your faith so that you could boldly proclaim who you are, claim your rights, and lead Christ where you wanted to go. It is little wonder that by the close of the 1980s we had become the *greed is good* and *you can have it all* culture. The Church had sold out to the culture. Even with all this shiny new *success*, the Church continued to decline. It was now competing with Wall Street and Multi-Level Marketing as a means of achieving a happy prosperous life. Instead of Eternal Life and a relationship with God, we were offering the same things that the devil offers.

Things have gotten worse. Apparently Jesus not only wants you to have a lot of money He also wants you to be beautiful and slim. We are now working out with Jesus and having a make-over with Jesus and eating healthy with Jesus. Anything that sells, sells better if you add Jesus to the mix. Discipleship that involves humility and a level of sacrifice and suffering may be godly and what Jesus requires, but unfortunately, it doesn't sell.

Growth

When I became a Senior Pastor in 1988 the Evangelical American Church was in the throes of the *Church Growth* movement. There were books and conferences galore promoting the notion *if you are not growing you are dying* and offering advice on how to become the next Willow Creek Church or Saddleback Church. Pastors were supposed to leave these conferences inspired to lead their church past the next growth barrier and at least reach a thousand in attendance, the mythical magic number for success. You didn't really need a vision from God, because that was already laid out for you. These conferences not only had the *what* they also had the *how*. You could be seeker-sensitive, or purpose-driven, or simply simple. Just choose one and go for it. More often most Pastors left confused and discouraged. Worse, many left headed in the absolute wrong direction. (For those who may still be trying to recover from all this mess I highly recommend reading *The Pastor* by Eugene Peterson.)

I am not saying that you shouldn't do things that may help your church grow. Of course you should try to make people feel welcome and do what you can to give the meeting place a good appearance. However, it isn't *your* church, and the idea that you should make your church grow is at the very start off-kilter. As a Pastor you have not been called to grow a church. You have been called to grow God's people. (Yes, I know I have already said that, but I don't think it can be said too many times.)

I personally bumbled around in this church growth idea for several years before I finally came to realize that breaking the next growth barrier and reaching a thousand was not the point. I grew up in a church of 120 and then went into the full time ministry in a church of 1,400. The last two years before coming to the church where I would Pastor for over thirty-two years, we attended a church of between four and five hundred. I loved that church for many reasons, not the least of which was its size. It was large enough to have the resources to do things but also small enough to still know virtually everyone. What finally got me out of the church growth maze was the Lord reminding me how much I loved that church and that I had basically told Him while we were still there that I wanted to Pastor a church that size. He had given me the desire of my heart, so why was I trying to replace the desire He gave me with one someone else was trying to tell me I was supposed to have?

My dad was a Pastor. He never Pastored over 120–150 people, but he was successful beyond his imagination. What my dad was great at doing was taking a small group of a dozen or so people in a not so affluent area and leading them to becoming a viable fellowship with godly influence in the community. It took sacrifice and hard work. I remember as a child going with my dad to the sawmill and to the concrete block business to get materials to build a meeting place. I remember the men of the church bringing their picks and shovels to hand dig the foundation. The women would show up around noon with lunch. He did this twice in two different small towns. There was little pay and virtually none of man's glory, but he wasn't doing it to make money or for man's praise. He had his eyes on a different kind of glory.

He has now gone on to be with the Lord. When I finally go as well, I'm not sure how many Celebrity Pastors will be in evidence, but I expect Harvey and Margaret Meek along with a host of other Pastors of *small* churches will have places of great honor. We do serve a King who declared that the first shall be last and the last first. Those who exalt themselves will be humbled, and those who humble themselves will be exalted.

I'm not saying that Pastors of large churches are wrong or bad people. What I am saying is that they are not our example. Know who God has called you to be. To some He gave five talents, to others two talents, and to others one talent. He doesn't reward us based on how many talents (or members, or commitment cards, or baptisms) we have. He rewards us based on whether or not we have been faithful. We do a grave disservice to Christ when we try to convince the person with one talent that he might as well go bury it in the ground because he doesn't have ten talents. No member of the Body of Christ can say to another, "I don't need you."

We also do a grave disservice when we try to move the church to focus on numbers and getting bigger. What you focus on overwhelms you, and you can't make two different things the central focus. The focus is and always truly must be on Christ.

I love the book of Colossians; especially these three passages:

The Son is the image of the invisible God, the firstborn over all creation. For in him all things were created: things in heaven and on earth, visible and invisible, whether thrones or powers or rulers or authorities; all things have been created through him and for him. He is before all things, and in him all things hold together. And he is the head of the body, the church; he is the beginning and the firstborn from among the dead, so that in everything he might have the supremacy. For God was pleased to have all his fullness dwell in him, and through him to reconcile to himself all things, whether things on earth or things in heaven, by making peace through his blood, shed on the cross. Colossians 1:15–20 (NIV)

(Christ) in whom are hidden all the treasures of wisdom and knowledge. Colossians 2:3 (NIV)

For in Christ all the fullness of the Deity lives in bodily form. Colossians 2:9 (NIV)

The kingdom of darkness rejoices when we turn our focus to anything that competes with Christ for our attention. Anything, no matter how important man thinks it is, that competes with Christ for our focus is clearly inferior and not what we have been called to lift up.

UNDERRATED UNITY

Some thirty years ago I was given a gift by one of the members of our congregation. It was a small polished stone with the word "Unity" embossed on it. Last year when I retired I passed that stone on to the young man taking my place of leadership in the church. Unity in the Body of Christ is grossly underrated in the American church culture.

Using the biblical analogy of the body to correspond with the Church the paramount importance of unity is plain. When someone is walking or moving, and their body isn't in sync, not only does it severely limit their ability to accomplish anything, but it is a sure sign that there is something wrong. Furthermore, when the parts of the body are fighting each other, we call that sickness.

What are the obstacles to unity?

There are any number of things that may hinder unity but I want to address three obstacles that I see as being primary.

- **Misunderstanding Unity Itself**

The Lord's Chapel in Brentwood, Tennessee, was of great

importance in my spiritual formation during my mid-twenties till my late thirties. It is the place where I first went into full time ministry as their Youth Pastor. When I became an Elder at The Lord's Chapel, I was surprised to learn that they had a standing unwritten rule that all votes by the Elders needed to be unanimous. In the swirl of the Charismatic renewal in the 70s this seemed to make sense. However, what was actually being said was that unanimity equals unity. This is simply not true. Unanimity is actually more of a sign of an unhealthy situation than a positive indicator.

In the early 80s Steve Taylor wrote a satirical song about church called "I Want to be a Clone." It was a song about becoming a Christian and entering *church life*. The title itself tells you the sense of the message. It was a prophetic word to the Church that was profoundly ignored. Later that decade comedian Jeff Foxworthy became famous for his "You Might Be A Redneck if..." routine. One that always made me laugh was, "You might be a redneck if your family tree doesn't fork." Well, you might be in an unhealthy church if everyone agrees about everything.

When I became a Senior Pastor and led a group of Elders at our church the rule was not that votes had to be unanimous, nor that a simple majority ruled. We strove for unity. There were times when I wanted to make some changes or move forward on a particular issue, and I had a significant majority of the Elders in favor. On those occasions we would step back and not move forward until we could reach, not unanimity, but unity.

Sometimes the point at question was simply tabled and often never again saw the light of day. An example involved a restructuring of the way Elders served. We considered Eldership to be a lifetime appointment. You weren't an Elder because you were serving a term in an elected office to help run the church. You were recognized as an Elder because you were already serving in that spiritual capacity in the church. A person could serve as an Elder in a spiritual leadership role, but that did not necessarily mean they should be required to attend regular frequent meetings.

I proposed that we allow Elders to decide each year whether to opt out of serving on the *Elder Board* because I could see burn out coming in several of the guys. For some reason a few of the Elders felt threatened by this proposition. Even though the majority were clearly for it, I let it drop to preserve unity. It was a good idea, but it was not at all a hill on which I was prepared to fight, much less die. (As a postscript most of the Elders who were opposed either resigned or moved away over the next two years. Burn out.)

Other times we would finally reach unity and move forward. An example of this involved bringing a woman on staff as the Assistant Pastor. I grew up in the Assemblies of God which had a tradition that allowed for a woman to be ordained and serve as a Pastor. We were bringing on our first Assistant Pastor, and I knew that God had chosen one particular lady to serve in that role. The objection some had was not about the ability of this lady to serve in this capacity but over using the word "Pastor" for her position. We already had a female *Children's* Pastor but apparently we could overlook that because these were children. When it came to adults, the term clearly bothered some of our Elders. I didn't drop this one. I felt that this lady was in fact going to be doing the work of a Pastor and needed to be recognized both for the authority such a title confers and because it was simply the right thing to do. After a couple of months of discussion we finally reached unity, and we now had a female Assistant Pastor. In this case I genuinely felt I had heard from God. This wasn't just a good idea.

Postscript to this event. Over twenty years later she is still serving in her role (though she is now called the Executive Pastor) and is greatly loved and respected in the church. Because we reached unity before making this move not only did we not lose any families when we brought on a female Pastor, but those Elders who were opposed have since acknowledged that she has made an excellent Assistant Pastor. I understand why some traditions believe that women should not serve as Pastors. I respect those traditions, but I don't agree with them.

So, what do I mean by unity if we are not talking about unanimity? It's quite simple. Unity is when you reach a point where, though some may not agree with a particular direction, all are willing to move together in that direction. Unanimity around anything other than the basic fundamental doctrines of the faith is usually a sign that your family tree doesn't fork. Unity that allows dissent is a sign that our unity in Christ overrules our (often petty) differences.

- **Misplaced Ambition**

There was a brother who came to me several years ago to tell me he wanted to be an Elder in the church. We'll call him Joe. Joe is a good man and one for whom I hold a great deal of respect and affection. The problem was that he was fairly easily offended. Christians in general are not supposed to take up offense, but for a leader taking offense can be particularly dangerous. Offense comes with the job description of being a leader. I told Joe this was my reservation about him, but I would bring his name before the Elders. All of the Elders knew Joe and basically shared my concerns. We discussed whether we should make Joe an Elder more than any other name that had ever come before us. We were bringing on a couple of other people, and we decided to not bring Joe on at this time. It was a test. If his reaction showed an ability to not take up offense we would bring him on soon after.

The day new Elders were announced and Joe was left off the list he got upset and stormed out right after service. One of the long time Elders went after him to calm him down, but Joe said some unkind words to this brother assuming that he had been one of those who were against making him an Elder. In fact, this brother had probably been Joe's strongest advocate. Joe left the church—but there is more.

A few years later Joe called me up and asked if we could meet. He wanted to come back to the church. Of course the door was wide open. Clearly there had been a change for the better in Joe.

Though Joe did not ask for it, several months later we invited him to be one of the Elders. He accepted, but a few years later he resigned because he recognized that serving as an Elders simply wasn't where he fit. Years later he is still at the church, and many people go to him for prayer and counsel. I told you he is a good man.

While some may desire a seat in the decision process while not understanding that they may not be cut out for it, there are others who have less noble motives. The ones who fall into this category are often not so much motivated by a desire serve as they are by an inflated sense of their own importance. They may not have overtly evil intent, but by simply being unwilling to follow the leadership of others they disqualify themselves from being a godly leader. The decisions become about them instead of what is best for others, or even what God has said. If such people are actually placed in leadership, you can pretty much forget about moving in true unity.

- **Misplaced Focus**

Most Christians are familiar with the Our Father which is often referred to as the Lord's Prayer. It is not the Lord's Prayer. This is the prayer Jesus taught the disciples to pray, so it is more accurate to call it the Disciple's Prayer. The Lord's Prayer is found in chapter 17 of John, and it is rich fertile ground for study. This is the prayer Jesus prayed in the hearing of His disciples on the night before going to the cross. It is among His very last words to His followers. One would expect this prayer to contain insight into what Jesus considered to be of the utmost importance. Verses 20–23 have always stood out to me.

"My prayer is not for them alone. I pray also for those who will believe in me through their message, that all of them may be one, Father, just as you are in me and I am in you. May they also be in us so that the world may believe that you have sent me. I have given them the glory that you gave me, that they may be one as we are one—I in them and you in me—so that they may be brought to complete unity. Then the

world will know that you sent me and have loved them even as you have loved me." John 17:20–23 (NIV)

Clearly Jesus is praying for those of us who were to come. He prays that we may be one and that we may be brought to complete unity. For those who may argue that being one denotes unanimity, I would point out that though Jesus always did what the Father commanded they did not always agree. On the night before the cross Jesus voiced His opinion. "I would rather not do this. Can't we find some other way?" In private Jesus expressed His opinion with the Father. In public, He moved in complete unity. Being *one* is not about unanimity, but rather about unity.

What really catches my attention here is what Jesus says will happen when we are one in complete unity. He specifically mentions two things. Twice He mentions that unity among believers will convince the world that Jesus was sent from God. He also says that the world will know that God loves them. Can you imagine how different things would be if the whole world already knew that Jesus came from God and that God loves them? These are the very things we are trying to get across to the world.

We put the message on billboards and broadcast it over the airways. We spend tremendous resources on training people to carry the message and then sending them with this wonderful news. We raise funds and hold conferences and crusades (*crusade* is an unfortunate word that is not ever going to resonate well in the Middle East) and set our best minds to strategize on the best way to spread this amazing news. At the end of the day we scratch our heads and wonder why there seems to be so little return for such a great investment. We conclude it must be because of the influence of the world. Of course that is a factor, but the real influence holding back the Gospel isn't the influence of the world so much as it is the influence of Christians.

Mahatma Gandhi is quoted as having said, "I like your Christ, I do not like your Christians. Your Christians are so unlike your Christ." There are those who would dismiss this because Gandhi was so tolerant of other faiths. They would claim that it is our job to defeat other faiths, and any believers who aren't doing that aren't real believers. The result is even less unity. I believe that no one comes to the Father except through Jesus, but I do not believe that I must destroy something else before I can point people to Christ. Jesus did not say if we destroy everything else people will finally come to Him. He said that if He is lifted up He will draw all people to Himself.

And There is More

Paul told the Church of the Colossians that he was praying for them, and he told them why. *My goal is that they may be encouraged in heart and united in love, so that they may have the full riches of complete understanding, in order that they may know the mystery of God, namely, Christ, in whom are hidden all the treasures of wisdom and knowledge.* Colossians 2:2–3 (NIV)

Unity is hard work. It is much easier to simply retreat into our own little circle and treat those with whom we disagree with either open hostility or benign neglect. At worst we criticize other camps of believers, but for the most part we just live and let live. They have their place, and we have ours. Even in the same fellowship where we may agree on doctrine and styles of worship we still tend to migrate to our own little cocoon. It is hard work welcoming strangers. It is hard work dealing with others who may make us uncomfortable. It is hard work staying put when we want to run. But seeing unbelievers come to know Christ isn't the only benefit of unity. Unity doesn't just helping others come to know Christ—it is also how we come to understand the mystery of God and have access to all the treasures of wisdom and knowledge.

Mark Twain has a wonderful quote about travel. "Travel is fatal to prejudice, bigotry, and narrow-mindedness, and many of our people need it sorely on these accounts. Broad, wholesome, charitable views of men and things cannot be acquired by vegetating in one little corner of the earth all one's lifetime." There is much truth in this quote, and the same principle applies to the Body of Christ. You can't really know much about Christ if everyone you hang out with is the same color, has the same mother tongue, votes for the same candidates, dresses the same, listens to the same music, reads the same translation, etc.

Our church has a theatre. I don't mean we do some *Church Plays*. We have a *theatre*, and we do popular plays that people know. We have tiered seating for 400 with great sight lines and a 60' x 40' proscenium stage with full stage rigging (except for a fly system) and ample wing space. We have a full scene shop for making sets and excellent lighting and sound abilities. Why do we have this? God told us to do it. During my years away from the Lord I got a degree in Theatre. When I came back to the Lord I laid the Theatre down because it was generally not the environment I needed to be in. On going into the ministry, and even years after becoming a Senior Pastor, the Theatre was simply not on my radar; however, once my children became teenagers and got interested in Theatre, the Lord just started sending people with a similar interest, and our plans to build a new ministry center with a gym morphed into a much better plan (for us) of building a theatre. I have discovered that often when we lay something down at the Lord's direction, the time may later come when He restores it to us far better than we could imagine.

We have reaped several great benefits from having a theatre in our church. On a practical level the facility needed to house a functional theatre is an excellent fit for housing worship services. As a result we have quite a bit of gear at our disposal for our worship services that was purchased by the theatre. Obviously other (mostly larger) churches have similar gear, but we get multiple use from it. On a *vision* level, the intent is outreach. People who would not be inclined to accept an invitation to a church service are often quite interested in attending a good quality production of *Fiddler on the Roof*, or *Anne of Green Gables*, or *Guys and Dolls*. The result is that they are often intrigued enough to come back on a Sunday and check out a service. They may not come to our church, but simply being *in* a church for such an experience may open them up to the notion of giving some other church a try. We've seen it happen fairly often. Additionally, we are totally open to having nonbelievers come and work on a show with us. They often find the process and atmosphere of doing a show with us to be life affirming in a way that they don't often find elsewhere. We've seen people come to Christ, or come back to Christ, through doing a show with us. Both of these outreach benefits were things I could foresee, but there was one other great benefit I did not see coming.

The majority of people in our productions are not from our church. In addition to unbelievers we have people from quite a few other churches who often work with us. We have people from a broad spectrum of denominations and worship styles. These are people who don't usually engage with one another in a setting where people freely talk about Jesus and their faith. The result is beautiful. As walls come down people discover that Jesus actually is present in other settings among other believers.

One more thing about our church. I never let politicks divide us. Our church is located in a firmly Red State. That means that our state almost always votes for the Republican Party. I intentionally don't bring politicks into the pulpit, though I have often been pressured to do so. I jealously try to keep the focus on Christ. The result is that we have both *Love it or Leave it* right wingers sitting next to *Pinko* left wingers along with even a few true independents. They know each other. They love each other. They deal with each other's views because the one thing that unites them is not where they may stand on current affairs, but Christ. It warms my heart because in doing so they are coming to the full riches of complete understanding and to know the mystery of God, namely, Christ, in whom are hidden all the treasures of wisdom and knowledge.

HUMILITY

In the 1960 musical *Camelot,* the Lancelot character is introduced by the song *C'est Moi.* The song is a funny spoof in which Lancelot claims to be answering the call of Camelot and the noble dream of a round table because it so clearly needs his singular mix of prowess and purity. He finally arrives at Camelot explaining why he is there and claiming to have never lost a joust. He is pulled up short when Queen Guenevere asks, "When did you last joust with humility?"

Humility is a baffling foreign concept to the bold knight. It is far too often a baffling foreign concept to *successful* Pastors. This is especially tragic when one considers that humility is not only an essential sign of the presence of the Holy Spirit in a person's life, but an absolute requirement for being a godly leader.

There should be little debate about who would be the two greatest leaders in the Bible. Obviously Jesus is the greatest, and the second greatest is almost as obvious. That would be Moses. I have always found it somewhat amusing that Moses himself wrote the book of Numbers, and in Numbers 12:3 we read the parenthetical statement, "Now Moses was a very humble man, more humble than anyone else on the face of the earth." Some people might consider it a paradox that someone who is truly humble would claim to be humble. Such people simply don't understand humility. Of course there are people who claim to be humble but are not. Still, humility isn't proved by bad mouthing one's self. Humility actually requires having a true measure of one's self.

What about Jesus? Was He humble? As was the case with Moses we can let Jesus speak to this Himself. In Matthew 11:29 Jesus says, "Take my yoke upon you, and learn of me; for I am meek and lowly in heart: and you shall find rest unto your souls." Meek is a synonym for humble. There you have it. The two greatest godly leaders of all time (one of whom was in fact God) and they both bear witness to being humble. So, can a truly great leader, a truly godly Pastor, *not* be humble?

Paul says in 2 Timothy 2:24–25, *"A servant of the Lord must not quarrel but be gentle to all, able to teach, patient, in humility correcting those who are in opposition."* (NIV) The culture in the United States tends toward admiring the bold brash leader who can tell it like it is without caring what anybody thinks. That is not a particularly admirable trait. Anyone crass enough or bully enough or psychotic enough can tell it like it is (from their narrow perspective) without caring what you, or anybody else, thinks. That is not a sign of one sent from God. The prophets of old often spoke boldly, but they cared a great deal about those to whom they were speaking (except for Jonah). The one prophet who was charged with bringing the hardest message was Jeremiah who was also know as the "Weeping Prophet."

Jesus certainly spoke truth boldly. He wasn't just speaking "his truth" but the very Truth of God, because He *was* God. The difference is that Jesus cared very deeply what others thought, not in a way that influenced His message, but because He cared so deeply for those to whom He was bringing the message. God is not willing that any should perish. Jesus' door was always open. Anyone who was willing to come to Him would never be turned away. Even more, Jesus would pursue and be persistent in His pursuit. He would even leave the ninety-nine to go after just the one lost sheep.

I have been listening to a *Christianity Today* podcast called "The Rise and Fall of Mars Hill." This podcast examines the quick rise and even quicker fall of a Seattle mega church, but it makes clear that this story isn't just about Mars Hill Church. The center of both the rise and fall of this church was a Pastor who was undeniably gifted and willing to shoot straight (usually) and unafraid to go against the culture. He even would sacrifice for certain groups of people, at least in the beginning. The problem was a severe deficiency of humility in the young man's life. He became too important in his own eyes. He could not learn anything from someone whose church wasn't larger than his. (I use the word *church* but it was more of a following than a true church.) Anyone who was even at all a perceived threat was dealt with harshly as the Pastor saw anyone who didn't agree with him was someone attacking God.

Think about that last sentence for a moment.

The situation at Mars Hill has been played out multiple times over the years, but it is magnified in an age of mega churches and social media. There are various factors that play into the fall of a local church, but one constant that seems to tie them all together is a lack of humility. Often this deficiency is centered in the lead Pastor, but it can also be at play in the Eldership, associate Pastors, and lay leaders. Any influential leader in the church who lacks humility can easily do a great deal of harm.

Of course there are times when correction and even discipline are necessary, but a leader without humility is a leader without the guidance of the Holy Spirit. The most ridiculous thing I ever heard a Pastor say (from the pulpit no less) was, "I'd rather be one step ahead of the Holy Spirit than one step behind Him." If you are even one inch ahead of the Holy Spirit then it is impossible to be led by Him. You are trying to lead Him. By the way, I was present when this Pastor made this statement, and he got a rousing "Amen" from the congregation. I'm not sure this is how you help form God's people into the likeness of Christ who was always led by the Holy Spirit.

Micah 6:8: *He has shown you, O mortal, what is good. And what does the LORD require of you? To act justly and to love mercy and to walk humbly with your God.* (NIV) Those who claim that they do walk humbly with God while walking proudly with their fellow man are either ignorant of, or willfully forgetting, the principle established in 1 John 4:20: *Whoever claims to love God yet hates a brother or sister is a liar. For whoever does not love their brother and sister, whom they have seen, cannot love God, whom they have not seen.* (NIV) Jesus made it clear that the way we treat others is the same as the way we treat Him.

It is not easy in our culture to lead from a place of humility. It is much easier to bully and lord it over others. However, Jesus specifically states that this is the way the Gentiles lead. I don't think He was making a racial statement by using the term *Gentiles*. I think He was saying that this is the way people without God lead. He goes on to say, *"Not so with you. Instead, whoever wants to become great among you must be your servant, and whoever wants to be first must be your slave—just as the Son of Man did not come to be served, but to serve, and to give his life as a ransom for many."* Matthew 20:26–28 (NIV)

Whenever you see a leader lording it over those following, you may be sure that they are not great in the sight of heaven no matter how big their *church* is, or how great their book sales, or what their press clipping may say. Also, they are not modeling Jesus. If you are charged to lead people to be like Jesus, then you must be willing to be like Jesus. Jesus was humble and lowly.

In your relationships with one another, have the same mindset as Christ Jesus: Who, being in very nature God, did not consider equality with God something to be used to his own advantage; rather, he made himself nothing by taking the very nature of a servant, being made in human likeness. And being found in appearance as a man, he humbled himself by becoming obedient to death—even death on a cross! Philippians 2:5–8 (NIV) It could not be much plainer than this. The result of this attitude on Christ's part was that God exalted Him to the highest place and gave Him a name above all names.

The other option is to decide to exalt oneself. This is of course exactly what the devil decided to do. Isaiah 14:13—*You said in your heart, "I will ascend to the heavens; I will raise my throne above the stars of God; I will sit enthroned on the mount of assembly, on the utmost heights of Mount Zaphon.* (NIV) The only way to be exalted by God is to walk in humility. 1 Peter 5:6—*Humble yourselves, therefore, under God's mighty hand, that he may lift you up in due time.* (NIV)

There is the way of Christ and the way of the world. The way of Christ always involves humility. Anyone who does not acknowledge this is either deceived or a deliberate deceiver.

GOALS

Proverbs 28:19 in the KJV says: *Where there is no vision, the people perish: but he that keepeth the law, happy is he.* Most new translations (including the New KJV) say, *Where there is no revelation, people cast off restraint; but blessed is the one who heeds wisdom's instruction.* In the American church many people know the first half of this verse while few know the later half. Unfortunately, most Christians who know this verse at all know it from the King James. The reason I say this is unfortunate is because it often leads people to ask their Pastor, "What is your vision?" I hated this question because it almost always gets we American Christians off track.

In my early 30s I attended a retreat with the Elders and Pastors of our church, The Lord's Chapel in Brentwood, Tennessee. The teaching was all about the need for vision. The speaker had been arranged by one of the staff Pastors with little input from the Senior Pastor. I went up to the Senior Pastor at the close of the retreat and asked him if he was going to share his vision with us. He replied, "I don't have one." He was a good man, but not a strong leader nor a deep thinker. He in fact did have a vision. His vision was both powerful and fruitful, and he had already shared it on several occasions, but this retreat had lead us to expect something called "fresh vision."

In our worldly success-driven American culture when, we hear the word *vision* we default to the notion of how to accomplish goals. For the Church these goals usually are about numeric growth and financial prosperity. They have to do with gaining worldly influence, presumably for God since obviously He wants us to have more worldly influence and needs our help to accomplish His plan. (Sarcasm alert.) This is a powerful, seductive trap and is a dangerous road to travel.

"Pastor, what is your vision for the church?" I hated that question, not because I didn't have the answer, but because the answer I had was not what the questioner was expecting, and usually not what he or she wanted to hear. What we want to hear is a clear road map for the church becoming bigger and more influential. We might say we want this so more people will be saved, and we do want more people to be saved, but that is secondary to obeying God. Getting more people saved is not the same thing as selling more cars or getting more subscribers to our offered service. If we just are getting more saved in a similar manner to adding to our multilevel marketing network it will be a house built on sand, and it will ultimately come unraveled. When our *works* are presented before God they will be proved by fire as only wood, hay, and stubble.

We not only want *fresh vision*, we want a *five-year plan*. We aren't just wanting to be told where we are going, but we also want to be in on exactly how we are going to get there. If you have actually read the Bible much you know that God doesn't always share *where* His people are going, and when He does He almost never shares *how* there are going to get there.

It has been my experience that vision is often a progressive thing. When I first came to the church in Smyrna, the vision I had been given was largely about being sort of a healing center for wounded Christians. We became that. As time went by there was a season when the local church vision grew to include a focus on the Arts. Several years ago my vision shifted to providing a healthy transition to the next generation of leadership. Now that I am retired, we have had a healthy transition to the next generation, but we continue to be a healing center, and we continue to have a strong Arts focus. All of this fits within the grand vision of Ephesians 4. We don't need a *new vision* for the overarching vision of the church. The Bible has given us a 2,000 year-old plan. God vision.

As a Pastor what is my vision for the church? *"To equip God's people for works of service, so that the body of Christ may be built up until we all reach unity in the faith and in the knowledge of the Son of God and become mature, attaining to the whole measure of the fullness of Christ. Then we will no longer be infants, tossed back and forth by the waves, and blown here and there by every wind of teaching and by the cunning and craftiness of people in their deceitful scheming. Instead, speaking the truth in love, we will grow to become in every respect the mature body of him who is the head, that is, Christ. From him the whole body, joined and held together by every supporting ligament, grows and builds itself up in love, as each part does its work."* Ephesians 4:12–16 (NIV)

Any Pastor who does not know Ephesians 4:12–16 is simply flying blind. They may appear to bear fruit, but it will not be fruit that will last. Entrepreneurs feel called to grow whatever catches their interest, including churches, but Pastors are not called to grow the church. Pastors are called to grow the people. In our culture many church *leaders* want a Pastor who will simply grow the church. Some want this because they truly see it as *getting more people saved*. Others want this because they would rather be a leader in a big influential church than in a small church. (I'm not judging anyone here, but each of us should judge our own heart and motives. If you need some help in understanding your motives, you might start with whether or not you have been offended by this paragraph.)

Let's go back to the retreat I mentioned earlier. My Pastor said he didn't have a vision. He was confused because we had just heard a compelling presentation about church growth. This is something that seems obvious in our culture, but also something God never called us to do. My Pastor led a church in the 70s and early 80s that had been the principle embodiment in our city of the Charismatic Renewal. His vision was that our church was to be a tunnel through which people passed and then went out bringing life and renewal to the Body of Christ all over the Nashville area and beyond. That is in fact what happened.

The Lord's Chapel no longer exists as a local church; however, the fruit of its vision is clearly evident in the greater Nashville area and well beyond. There are several churches that grew to become larger than the Chapel that were helped greatly by members from the Lord's Chapel. There are at least three strong churches in the area that received significant blessing from the Chapel in terms of financial resources. Many other churches were blessed and renewed by the influence and leadership of those who we often referred to as "Chapel Graduates."

Please allow me to paraphrase Proverbs 28:19 in a fashion specific to the local church. "Where the vision is messed up with a secular focus you ultimately find a mass grave of shipwrecked faith, broken relationships, and needless painful hurt. But where the vision is based on God's biblical instruction for what the church should be there is joy in bearing fruit that will last."

WHEN PEOPLE LEAVE

People are going to leave the church where you Pastor. Some of them will be people you never actually knew were attending the church, but others will be people you thought were in for the long haul. Some may even be people you considered to be close friends. Make no mistake, there will be some people you will not be too broken up to see go, but that will not often be the case. When (not if) people leave, here are some things to keep in mind.

It's Not Your Church

The good thing about knowing that it is not your church is that since it is God's Church He will take care of things no matter how devastated you may feel when losing people.

It was 1995, and we had been at the church for seven years. We had grown from around 50–60 to around 200. The men had just been to a Promise Keepers event in Atlanta, so there was quite a bit of buzz and energy among our guys. The speaker who had impacted me the most at this event was Tony Evans. He had some powerful things to say about racial issues. I had always felt that race was a huge embarrassment of the American Church. It was almost a renunciation of the Kingdom of God to be so chronically, intentionally, and stubbornly segregated in our churches. I had also always wanted our church to be multi-ethnic and multi-racial. A couple of Sundays after Promise Keepers I brought a sermon on the sin of racism. All seemed well, and then I got the letter.

I received a well written missive from one of our families outlining why I was wrong because each race has their place and God does not intend for us to mix. Therefore, this young couple would be leaving the church. Let's call them Bob and Betty Smith. (Not their real names.) We were not extremely close, but we were certainly good friends. They were near the same age as my wife and I. Bob and I played softball together. My wife and I had shared meals with them on several occasions. Overall I expected us to grow in friendship for many years to come. I was disappointed, but there were no hard feelings; however, that wasn't the only reason I was disturbed at their leaving.

I am ashamed to admit this, but it is honest, and every Pastor who is honest will be able to identify. The Smiths were probably among the top five tithers in the church. As with most young churches we were usually living month to month financially (at least we had gotten past the week-to-week phase). It was also mid-summer which, as most Pastors know, generally signals a lull in giving. One of my first thoughts was, "What are we going to do without their giving?" The Lord convicted me of both my lack of faith in Him and feeling like I was looking at people as giving units rather than His people. All I could do was fall back on the reality that it is not my church. I repented and waited. I didn't have long to wait. Once they left the church, giving essentially shot up.

It didn't have anything to do with something wrong on the part of the Smiths. They had never used their giving to try and influence any decisions. They never actually mentioned their giving. Additionally, we didn't change anything in terms of the way we received offerings or tried to increase our appeal for giving. I believe it basically had to do with God teaching me a lesson. It is His Church. He is the source. He will take care of things.

Don't Burn Bridges

In my over 32 years as the Pastor at our church there has only been one occasion when I asked someone to leave. This occasion involved a man who simply would not leave some of the women alone. There was this one recently widowed lady to whom he was particularly attracted. He even went so far as to tell her that her husband (with whom he was only mildly acquainted) had told him to take care of her. I brought him face to face with a couple of the ladies who were complaining about him. When they outlined his abusive behavior he flat out said that they were lying. They were not lying. Did I mention that he was also married? I also learned that he was asked to leave his prior church for the same behavior. Obviously, I'm willing to go pretty far with people before cutting ties, but I do draw the line at predatory behavior.

I'm sure we have had hundreds of people leave over the years, but only perhaps a score of families with whom I had personal involvement in their leaving. Not many people will actually talk to you before leaving, so you have little idea why they left, or in some cases even if they have left. With the one exception I just described there is not one person I can think of who has left who would not be welcomed back. There are some I would keep a pretty close eye on if they returned, but they would still be welcome. Perhaps even more important is the fact that in our small town of around 60,000 there isn't anyone who has left our church who I would be hesitant to run into out in public. The last time I saw the Smiths (mentioned earlier) I was ordering at a fast food restaurant, and when they saw me they insisted on buying my lunch and invited me to sit and eat with them (which I gladly did).

Sometimes People Are Supposed To Leave

Not everyone belongs at the church where you are the Pastor. That may come as a revelation, but I can assure you that it is true.

Some shouldn't be at your church because they have disagreements or maybe just a bad attitude that will hurt others. The writer of Hebrews tells us to make every effort to live at peace with everyone and then goes on to say, *"See to it that no one falls short of the grace of God and that no bitter root grows up to cause trouble and defile many."* Hebrews 12:15 (NIV). Some people need to leave because if they stay they will "defile many." They may not be bad people. They simply have such strong issues with the leadership and direction of the church that they cannot help but create discord. They need to be somewhere else.

This does not mean that it is OK to burn bridges with these people. Attitudes change. Hearts change. I've had several people who left with not so great attitudes who later came back with a completely different perspective. Had bridges been burned that could not have happened.

One case in particular involved a Worship Pastor I let go. Let's call him George. The reasons why I let George go were complicated, and frankly I was sorry to have to do it. He and his wife were quality people. When the new Worship Pastor came in they stayed around for a short while but were just too wounded to stay. They left and went elsewhere for a few years and finally moved out of town. Before moving they came back to the church for a short while, and it was healthy for both them and the church. George now stops by often to see me when he is traveling through our area. One of the most cherished moments I've had as a Pastor was one day when George said to me, "When we left I thought you had done me pretty wrong, but now I see you actually did the best you could by me." I'm not sure I actually did the best I could, but it brings sweet tears to my eyes just remembering him saying this. Don't burn bridges, even with those who leave under less that ideal terms.

Pruning

Some people shouldn't be at your church because God wants them elsewhere. Concerning His Father, Jesus said, *"He cuts off every branch in me that bears no fruit, while every branch that does bear fruit he prunes so that it will be even more fruitful."* John 15:2 (NIV)

Local churches are not intended to become bloated fat organisms. If your church is really fruitful, I don't think that will necessarily show up in attendance numbers or your bank account. It will show up because people are being matured in Christ. As they mature there will be those who need outlets for serving in ministry. If you have more anointed and ready worship leaders or teachers or simply good faithful people than you need, that doesn't always mean you should add more services or *franchise* your brand. It may mean there is another church, perhaps not too far away, that really needs some of these people. If God chooses to send them elsewhere, He certainly has the right to prune fruitful branches.

In 2017 two of our long serving staff Pastors retired. These guys were quite popular, and not everyone was pleased with their retiring. We also had a third of our Elders leave and some prominent worship team members. Additionally, several of our young leaders I was grooming left around this time. Here is what happened.

One of the young leaders who left went to a small Presbyterian Church. The people were so impressed with him that they helped send him to seminary where he is studying to become a minister. Another got involved with a young church plant where he has become a best friend (and a strong encouragement) to the young Pastor. The prominent worship team people went to a small Baptist Church to help a new Pastor trying to revitalize the congregation and where they have now been faithfully leading worship for several years. The Elders who left have gone to other places and have fruitful ministry and influence for the kingdom.

What happened in our church is exactly what Jesus said would happen after pruning. Overall we have gotten both younger and stronger. The Worship Ministry is as strong or stronger than ever. The Elders as a whole are revitalized and stronger than ever as new ones have stepped into roles for which they were prepared. To say that these areas are stronger is no slap at what and who came before. Far from it. It is a testimony to who came before. This is what is supposed to happen. Our long time Worship Pastor laid a great foundation. Our former Elders set an example from which the new Elders greatly benefited. Sometimes people need to leave because God is pruning a fruitful branch. The church as a whole should be moving from glory to glory.

It Isn't Personal

When people leave it can be difficult to not take it as a personal rejection of you as the Pastor. Most of the time this is not the case. Believe it or not people have other reasons than you for the decisions they make. I'm not saying that to throw it in anyone's face. I'm saying it because I know from personal experience that it takes years to realize this. I'm just trying to plant a seed to help others get there easier. There is a lot of freedom in knowing that even though you may think otherwise, it is probably not about you at all.

What if it is about you? Then you are in good company. Moses struggled with people who made it clear they did not want to follow his lead. Samuel was so focused on thinking it was about him that the Lord had to tell him straight up, "They are not rejecting you. They are rejecting me." It turns out that Samuel wasn't God. I'm not either. You're not either. Jesus is God, but even He experienced this. Anyone who has been a Pastor long enough can totally identify with how Jesus felt when He turned to His disciples after bringing a challenging sermon that caused many to abandon Him and asked, "Do you want to leave me also?"

If it is about you then first of all you need to honestly ask God, "Why?" Sometimes the person leaving can tell you why, but often they may be off the mark. God is the only one who really knows, and if you are humble enough to learn, He will share this information with you. Have I missed my calling somewhere? Is there something I'm not seeing, something I'm not doing or something I am doing, that isn't pleasing (not to people) but to God? The first week I was a Youth Pastor I went to visit a friend of mine on the other side of town who had become a Youth Pastor a couple of years prior. I'll never forget what she said to me that day. "Once you learn how to do this job, you are finished." It is so easy to *learn* how to do this job. Once we *learn* how to do the job then gradually, without even noticing, we are no longer listening to God. Sometimes people leaving is God getting our attention.

The other thing we need to realize is that just because it is about me doesn't mean that I have missed the mark. People are people. Abraham Lincoln was not wrong when he said, "You can please some of the people some of the time, all of the people some of the time, some of the people all of the time, but you can never please all of the people all of the time." Beyond that it is not our job to please people. It is our job to help mature the body of Christ, the people of God. Part of that maturing process will involve some people not liking you because of a decision you made. Understand that sometimes them not liking you may simply be a part of their maturation process and part of your job description.

Important Note

Carrying the burden of thinking you are always at fault, or walking in the arrogance of thinking you are never at fault, are two drop offs on either side of the path you walk as a Pastor. They will both kill you and damage others around you. This is why you have to walk humbly with God.

MONEY, SEX, POWER
AND THE REAL MINISTRY KILLER

Pastors fall and ministries fail. This does not mean there is something wrong with God's plan, or that God isn't able. It means that people are people. We may be redeemed, but we are still imperfect people living in a fallen world. We are still subject to temptation. Some temptations are obvious, but some are devilishly subtle. Many people leave the ministry every year for various reasons. Often the reasons have to do with a fall.

The Big Three

- **Money**

The vast majority of Pastors do not get rich. Many have to be bi-vocational to simply make ends meet. Nevertheless, money continues to be the Achilles' heel of many Pastors from both ends of the line. The standing joke among the Pastors I grew up around was that most congregations had the attitude, "Lord, you keep him humble, and we'll keep him poor." There was, and often still is, a lot of truth in that *joke*.

My dad was always bi-vocational. He worked as a butcher in

a local grocery and sold shoes in a local retail shoe store. When I was three years old he came to a small community in rural Middle Tennessee just north of Nashville. Millersville was not the sort of place one boasted of being from, but as I look back on my childhood it was a pretty sweet rural setting convenient to a good-sized city. He took a congregation of a dozen people meeting in a rented one room building (with a damp basement) in an area of town called Dogpatch and over the next sixteen years led them to a church of 120 with their own building on the major highway that ran through the community. He started out making $35 a week plus his electric and phone bill being paid each month. I'm not sure exactly when they raised his salary, but it was approximately ten years after taking the church when he was increased to $50 a week plus his electric and phone bill being paid each month. Granted, a dollar was worth a good bit more in terms of what it would buy in those days, but still. I believe $50 weekly was still his salary when he was fired at a church business meeting after sixteen years of fruitful and sacrificial service. I'm not bitter, and I don't know that he was (at least he never showed it to me), but his story is not all that uncommon.

When Pastors are in such situations it is usually at a small church where they serve several functions, often including managing the church finances. The temptation can be strong to occasionally take a little extra. After all, they truly are seriously underpaid, and they can have unexpected emergencies arise. I was too young to be certain, but I am reasonably confident that my dad never did this, but I am absolutely certain that it does happen. When it happens, even if no one finds out, what it does is like stage four cancer to the integrity of the ministry and an unrelenting ache in the heart of the Pastor involved. I suspect most Pastors in such situations don't steal. They simply leave the ministry because the financial pressures on their families are so great.

The other end of the line is where the Pastor does become rich in this world's wealth. This has always been an issue, not just for the Church, but with virtually every religion known to mankind. Religion is one of the easiest ways to separate people from their money, and where there is money to be made you will always find scammers and the unscrupulous. This is particularly the case in the current American church where there is actually teaching that God wants you (and of course me) to be rich, rich, rich!

Paul wrote to Timothy and told him that those who want to be overseers should not be "lovers of money." He goes on to say, *"Those who want to get rich fall into temptation and a trap and into many foolish and harmful desires that plunge people into ruin and destruction."* 1 Timothy 6:9 (NIV) If this is the case with those who want to get rich, what about those whose ministry is to encourage others to want to get rich? He told Timothy that there will terrible times in the last days. He listed what will make the times terrible, and the first two thing he says are that people will love "themselves" and "money."

It is a dangerous thing for Pastors to become rich through the ministry. Shortly before becoming a Senior Pastor I was told about a Pastor who decided to only take up designated offerings in their church. Every tithe and offering was to be designated by the giver. Surprise! His salary shot up with this new policy. I was advised that this might be a good thing to do. There are so many things wrong with this suggestion that it is hard to know where to begin. From the tax code issues to the lack of any biblical reference for this manner of giving there are issues on top of issues. Perhaps the greatest issue is the trap it creates for the Pastor. Of course most of the giving goes to the person in the pulpit each week. Other ministries in the church suffer while the Pastor rakes it in. All the while this is being done under the guise of allowing the people *freedom*. What a sweet cover for greed.

In the 1970s there was a rock band with a Christian emphasis called Daniel Amos. It was an appropriate name because they really were a prophetic voice to the Church and the Culture. One song in particular I remember was called *I Didn't Build It For Me*. The song goes on to mention the plaque on the wall with the singer's name and also the statue of his family in the lobby. But of course he never would have done it had it not been for the *vision*. It may be a little over the top, but it is certainly not far from the truth.

It is so easy once the money ball starts rolling for a Pastor (or any religious leader) to stand back, wash their hands like Pilate, and claim they have nothing to do with this. This is simply God blessing them, and they are powerless to stop it. There are words I could apply to such a disclaimer, but they are not words I'm going to put in this book. I will just remind us all what Paul said about those who want to get rich. They follow harmful desires that plunge them into ruin and destruction. The money may continue to flow, the so called *ministry* may continue to function, but the actual ministry died long before it is buried. Money is one of the Big Three ministry killers.

• **Sex**

You don't have to be handsome to be a rock star with groupies. In the same way you don't have to be handsome to be a Pastor with certain access to the allure of immoral sex. Virtually anyone in a position of authority has an allure that some others will find attractive. This is especially true if that position of authority carries with it a *holy* veneer. Rock stars attract some not just because they are up front but also because they usually have the image of *bad boys* (or girls). Pastors are the other side of the coin and are not only up front but also have the image of being the *good man* for which some are truly longing.

Every Pastor needs to be aware that there are forces at work in illicit sexual allure that are unique to their calling. They are *famous* within their circle of influence. They are someone's dream because they are so *close to God*. When you preach what is right, people can't help but imagine that you yourself always get it right in your life. In addition to these two strong attractions, there is the fact that you often encounter people when they are at their most vulnerable emotionally. People come to their Pastor when they have experienced tragedy, loss, or heart break. You are that sympathetic ear they need, that source of encouragement, that shoulder on which to cry. It is a small step to become the arms in which to fall.

There is also the fact that in addition to the regular ups and downs that all marriages face, Pastors and their wives often have a unique set of pressures in their relationship—I will address this deeper in the chapter on families. The Pastor is going through a rough stretch at home. The vulnerable person they are *counseling* is attracted to them. The next thing you know they fall, the ministry falls, life itself starts to crumble. This is not inevitable, but it is all too common.

In the 1980s there were some headline-making situations of this sort involving celebrity Pastors. Jim Bakker and Jimmy Swaggart were the two most famous examples. Both were Assemblies of God ordained ministers. This is not a slap at the Assemblies of God, just a statement of fact. I was in Zimbabwe at the time teaching in an Independent Bible School for Pastors, but several of the folks there knew I had a background with the Assemblies. Bakker had already had his credentials revoked, and the issue was what they would do with Swaggart since he was pouring massive contributions into the Assemblies. I had several suggest to me that the Assemblies would go easy on him in order to keep the money flowing. I told them there was no way they would not discipline him money or no money. I was right.

Shortly after the fall of Bakker and Swaggart we had a couple from the States come and visit us in Zimbabwe. He was a Pastor friend that I had know for over ten years, and my wife and I had grown close to this couple. Let's call him Sam (not his real name). Sam and I were close in age, and while I was not yet Pastoring a church and not affiliated with the Assemblies, he was currently Pastoring an Assemblies of God church in the western suburbs of Chicago. Additionally, both Sam and I had grown up in the home of an Assemblies of God Pastor.

The topic of Bakker and Swaggart came up, and he informed me that these were not the only ones who had fallen because of moral failure. Apparently one of the Executive Presbyters of the General Council of the Assemblies of God had also fallen. This man wasn't well-known enough to make national headlines, but he was certainly known enough in the Assemblies to be a national figure within the denomination. We shook our heads and discussed how in the world this could happen. Well-known, respected leaders in the church were falling into sexual sin. Didn't they know this was wrong? Didn't they see this coming?

A few years later, after I had become the Pastor of our church in Smyrna, Tennessee, we had a young couple start attending our church who had a connection to Sam's church. The wife's mother was a member of Sam's church in Chicago. I was delighted to get to know them and have them at our church. A few months later they informed me on a Sunday morning that Sam had resigned his church. The previous Sunday he had announced to the congregation that he had been seeing a prostitute and was leaving his wife.

How could he do this? There are actually as many different answers to that question as there are people who have fallen. What is clear is that this could happen to anyone. If it could happen to Sam, it could happen to me. If it could happen to me, it could happen to you. The fact that this did not happen to me doesn't give me the right to sit in the place of judgment, but it should serve as a cautionary tale.

What can you do to keep from falling to sexual temptation? I could give you some hints from my own experience, but I really don't know how helpful that would be. Everyone is different. What I would encourage you to do is seriously consider 1 Corinthians 10:12–13 (NIV).

So, if you think you are standing firm, be careful that you don't fall! No temptation has overtaken you except what is common to mankind. And God is faithful; he will not let you be tempted beyond what you can bear. But when you are tempted, he will also provide a way out so that you can endure it.

There are three things about temptation that you must know.

1. No temptation has come to you except what is common to mankind. There are only three bullets in the tempter's gun: the lust of the flesh (money), the lust of the eyes (sex), and the boastful pride of life (power). This is what Eve was tempted with in the Garden. This was what Jesus was tempted with in the wilderness by the devil. It is what we are all tempted with. Your's is not a special case.

2. When you are tempted God will always provide a way of escape. In the case of sexual temptation it is usually the wisdom to not put yourself in compromising positions. As a last resort the way of escape is to simply leave. There is the door. Use it to walk out.

3. When you think you are standing firm is when you are the most likely to fall.

That last piece of information is probably the most important. It really needs no unpacking. It just needs to be seared into our consciousness. I am always liable to fall. I never reach the point where I am beyond falling.

I remember an Elder's meeting at the Lord's Chapel when one of the older Elders shared that as a young believer he asked an older man if there was ever a time when he would stop noticing the young women. The older man had told him it was age 65. He was in his late 60s at the time and told us that night, "I'm here to tell you it isn't 65." One of the other Elders joked, "It's 85." I'm not 85 yet, but I feel pretty confident in saying that it isn't 85 either.

• **Power**

There are times as a Pastor when you feel powerless. This is especially true for those who Pastor a small church, which is the case for the vast majority of Pastors. You can't make people attend services. (As Yogi Berra says, "If people don't want to come to the ballpark how are you going to stop them?") You can't make people listen to your sermons. You certainly can't make the ones who do listen to your sermons like them. Virtually everyone who serves in the church is a volunteer, so you don't have any financial authority over them as is the case in running a business. In fact, the opposite seems true. They have financial authority over you.

Perhaps this feeling of powerlessness is the reason why some Pastors tend to act as if they have a great deal of power. Maybe they feel they have something to prove? As a result they can become harsh with the people even though the Scripture specifically says to not do this. They will cast people out for minor offenses. They will tend to make people feel that their relationship to the local church (and perhaps even the Pastor) is the equivalent of their relationship with God. As a result when things go sour for folks at church, they have trouble understanding that God still loves them, or perhaps even that He ever did love them.

This situation often becomes even more extreme when the church grows to the point where the Pastor actually does have such standing that he, or she, is able to call the shots. They have paid staff who need the Pastor's favor in order to keep their jobs. They have such support from the congregants that anyone with a dissenting opinion about anything is a target for ridicule and censorship. They tend to think that they are the Moses figure; not the real Moses, but the one in the movies.

There is case after case of large churches and small churches falling apart because the Pastor felt the need to exercise his or her power.

First of all it is important to understand that it is not your church. I recently had a conversation with a faithful member of a large church organization. She was saying how some of the younger leaders were saying the church was going to have to change if it is going to survive. I called time out in the conversation and said, "How many times in the past 2,000 years has that been said? It is not up to people to make the Church survive." The Church belongs to God, and He will see to its survival. The church belongs to God, and you are not God. You have the privilege of working for Him, but you are a sharecropper, not a landowner. God doesn't need you. You need Him.

There are examples in Scripture of godly leaders exercising power, but it is never for their own benefit. Here are some scriptures that directly address how a leader in the church should conduct themselves.

And the Lord's servant must not be quarrelsome but must be kind to everyone, able to teach, not resentful. Opponents must be gently instructed, in the hope that God will grant them repentance leading them to a knowledge of the truth. 2 Timothy 2:24–25 (NIV)

Not that we lord it over your faith, but we work with you for your joy, because it is by faith you stand firm. 2 Corinthians 1:24 (NIV)

Jesus said to them, "The kings of the Gentiles lord it over them; and those who exercise authority over them call themselves Benefactors. But you are not to be like that. Instead, the greatest among you should be like the youngest, and the one who rules like the one who serves." Luke 22:25–26 (NIV)

Those who feel the need to often exercise their power almost always do so to defend their position. This is not the example Jesus set. This is not how God would have us lead. This is why the fruit turns rotten and for the sake of the Kingdom of God such leaders actually need to fall. Those who don't fall continue on in their error establishing cults and ungodly patterns that do much harm.

The Big One

There is actually one other thing that I believe destroys more ministries than anything else. It can often manifest itself as one of the Big Three, but it is more subtle and more basic. It isn't the lust of the flesh, the lust of the eye, or the boastful pride of life—though it has its roots in all three and forms a foundational antithesis to faith.

Insecurity

Insecurity causes us to abuse authority because deep inside we are afraid we will lose our position. It causes us to feel the need to create the illusion of success to prove that we are really God's man or woman. It causes us to look elsewhere for fulfillment. Popularity, money, sex, pride, self righteousness, all become substitutes for the genuine presence of God in our lives, because we don't fully trust Him to take care of us, we don't fully trust the call He has given us, we don't fully trust Him to set all things right.

Saul was the first king of Israel. He had no dynasty because he was insecure which leads to being fearful. In fact, he had three fears chronicled in Scripture that ended up costing him everything.

- **One**

In 1 Samuel 13 we read about Saul and Israel facing the Philistines. The Philistines were assembled to fight against Israel, but Saul was supposed to wait for Samuel to come and offer the sacrifice to the Lord before they could fight. Samuel was late in coming, and because the men of Israel saw that they were greatly out-numbered they began to desert the army leaving Saul in a worse and worse situation. Finally Saul decided to offer the sacrifice himself. Why? He was afraid of the enemy. That is a fear we can understand, but we don't have to buy into it. If our trust is in ourselves we will buy into it, but if our trust is in the Lord then the enemy doesn't stand a chance.

As soon as Saul finished offering the sacrifice Samuel arrived. "What have you done?" Samuel asked. Saul explained that he felt compelled to offer the sacrifice because he was afraid of the enemy. That fear cost him his dynasty.

"You have done a foolish thing," Samuel said. "You have not kept the command the LORD your God gave you; if you had, he would

have established your kingdom over Israel for all time. But now your kingdom will not endure; the LORD has sought out a man after his own heart and appointed him ruler of his people, because you have not kept the LORD's command." 1 Samuel 13:13–14 (NIV)

• **Two**

In 1 Samuel 15 Saul is given a seemingly easy assignment. He is charged with going to destroy the Amalekites. He is to kill them all and also destroy all of their animals. This was apparently a fairly easy victory; however, Saul did not obey what God told him to do. He allowed Agag, the king, to live. He also allowed the best of the sheep, cattle, fat calves, and lambs to be spared. They did destroy everything that was weak and despised.

When Samuel came on the scene Saul made excuses saying that he did follow the Lord's orders in spite of the obvious evidence that he did not. *"But I did obey the LORD," Saul said. "I went on the mission the LORD assigned me. I completely destroyed the Amalekites and brought back Agag their king. The soldiers took sheep and cattle from the plunder, the best of what was devoted to God, in order to sacrifice them to the LORD your God at Gilgal."* 1 Samuel 15:20–21 (NIV)

This was occasion when Samuel gave the famous quote, "To obey is better than sacrifice."

The result of Saul's unfaithfulness here was that the Lord rejected him as king. It didn't happen that moment—just as Adam and Eve did not physically die on the day they fell—but just because it doesn't happen right away doesn't mean it wasn't a fait accompli. Why did Saul do this? Saul explains it plainly in verse 24. *"I have sinned. I violated the LORD's command and your instructions. I was afraid of the men and so I gave in to them."* (NIV)

We can understand Saul being afraid of the enemy, but it is perhaps even more important for those in the ministry to be aware of the fear that caused God to reject him as king. He was afraid of his own people. His fear of the people rendered him unable to obey God. Insecurity causes Pastors to be particularly vulnerable to this fear. It is a fear that is easy to rationalize. The people wanted to sacrifice to God. Surely God can't be displeased with that? Actually, He can.

Pastors who are insecure will either give in and basically let the people lead themselves, or they will overreact and claim to be the sole mouthpiece through which God can speak to the fellowship. They let the people lead because they feel threatened. They overreact because they feel threatened. I had a Pastor who would basically side with whoever was the last to speak to him. He was the embodiment of Proverbs 18:17 *In a lawsuit the first to speak seems right, until someone comes forward and cross-examines.* (NIV) The result was that you could never really trust his decision about anything, because it might change tomorrow based on who he last talked with. I had another Pastor who was always right, even when he wasn't. Both situations are symptoms of insecurity.

Our security does not come from being popular with the people. That can change in a flash. Our security does not come from having a majority support on the Church Board. Our security does not come from having an iron-clad contract. Our security does not come from our talent, intelligence, or tenure. Our security comes from walking humbly with the Lord. It is His Church, and He is in charge. If He doesn't want you to be the Pastor anymore then you shouldn't be. If He does want you to be the Pastor then there is nothing man do about it.

When you have this security it allows you to do two things. When you know that you have heard from God you take responsibility as a called leader and do what God has told you regardless of what others want or may think. You understand that you don't necessarily hear directly from God on every issue. When you miss it, and unless you are perfect you will miss occasionally, you punt. You aren't afraid to admit that you missed it. (News Flash! You aren't perfect. You will occasionally miss it. If you don't recognize this then you are delusional.)

• Three

David. The chronology concerning David can be a little confusing from 1 Samuel 16 on to the end of the book. Nevertheless, a couple of things are crystal clear. The Lord's anointing was on David. David was a great blessing to Saul's reign. Saul was afraid of David because David was so successful, and it was evident that he carried God's anointing. In other words, Saul's third fear was being afraid of the anointing of God on someone else's life.

Had Saul not feared David there is little doubt that his own kingdom and family would have been far more successful. But Saul *was* afraid of David. He was afraid that David would take his place and that his dynasty would not endure. First of all God had already said that Saul's dynasty would not endure, but Saul did not have the kind of relationship with God that made him willing to accept what God had said. Someone is going to take your place. You may have an idea of who you want it to be and when you want it to be. Others may have an idea of who and when it should be. But the only one who truly matters in choosing your replacement and its timing is God. It is His Church.

The priest Eli is a mixed bag as a leader. (Aren't we all?) He erred greatly by not disciplining his sons and allowing them to bring the worship of the Lord into disrepute. However, he did get two things absolutely right. First, he was able to help Samuel recognize the voice of the Lord. Perhaps more importantly when the word of the Lord came to Samuel saying that the guilt of Eli's house will never atoned for by sacrifice or offering Eli replied, "He is the Lord; let Him do what is good in His eyes."

I mentioned earlier the worship Pastor I had to let go. He and his wife stayed at the church a couple of months after the new worship Pastor came on staff. In fact, they worked under him for those couple of months helping on the worship team. I had high hopes that they were going to really grow under his leadership, and I knew they could be a great help for him. When they did finally leave they said to the new guy, "If we aren't leading worship here there is no reason for us to be here." He wisely said to them, "That is why you aren't leading worship here." If you aren't willing to be in second or third place you aren't ready to be in first place.

When you enter a position as a Pastor you should do so with the understanding that your tenure will be temporary. You may hold your position for a few months or a few decades. In either event you will not hold it forever. If you are to serve well you will understand that it is not about you and how long you can hold on. The person who is concerned with holding their position will be subject to all of the errors caused by insecurity. The person who is at peace with being fully aware that this position is not their's to keep, but that it will either end with them (often not a good sign of success) or will pass on to someone else who is inherently more secure in their calling.

Saul was insecure, and so he saw David as a threat. Had he been willing to help David it could have been a great blessing—to Israel and to both David and Saul. Instead, Saul spent much time, energy, and resources trying to kill David. In doing so he weakened the kingdom and himself spending many sleepless nights of worry and anxiety.

If you are having trouble making the connection here, let me spell it out clearly. If you are a Pastor, the odds are great that the Lord will send you younger leaders in the church. A big part of your job is to train and prepare these younger leaders. By doing so they become a great blessing to the church and ultimately to the kingdom. Occasionally one of these young leaders will clearly be special. They may not be the most talented or the most charismatic (or maybe they will be), but they will obviously have the favor and anointing of the Lord on them. A secure Pastor will look for opportunities to test them and to open doors for them to serve. An insecure Pastor will look for ways (however subtle) of holding them back; perhaps even overtly discoursing them. An insecure Pastor will work to undermine the credibility of the younger leader. Perhaps none of this will be blatant until the time clearly comes for the younger leader to step up and take charge. When that time comes, the Pastor will refuse to step aside. That is the time to start writing the obituary for that church and for that Pastor's fruitful ministry.

If you are depending on yourself and your talents, popularity, knowledge, or any other human traits then you will be insecure. If you are depending on God and truly believe that He is in charge, that He has you regardless of circumstances, then you can be fearless. A truly humble fearless Pastor is a great gift to the kingdom of God.

FAMILY

In 1984 the movie *Footloose* was released. The plot concerned a small town where dancing was illegal within the city limits. It is actually based in part on true events from Elmore City, Oklahoma. The lead character is Ren McCormack who moves to this small town from Chicago. Ren is amazed that the seniors at the local high school are unable to have a Senior Prom dance because of the ridiculous local ordinance. A local influential Pastor is a firm supporter of the ordinance and the main roadblock to getting it changed. This Pastor has a daughter, Ariel, who becomes the main love interest and unsurprisingly disagrees with her dad's position about things. At one point in the movie Ren is talking to his best buddy, Willard, about Ariel and her *date life*. The conversation concludes with Willard observing, "I think she trying to make people forget she is a preacher's kid." Every PK (Preacher's Kid) who saw the movie had a sudden intake of breath at that line.

Growing up in the Pastor's home can be difficult. In fact, it almost always is difficult. It is almost as difficult as being a Pastor's wife. One of the most important things a Pastor has to do is to be there for his family and protect them. This can be said about any husband and father, but there are some unique challenges that are added to the mix when you are a Pastor. If things are crumbling at home, it is only a matter of time before everything else falls apart.

What Is Your Relationship To The Church?

I once heard the five ministries listed in Ephesians 4 being explained by comparison to the hand. The Apostle is the thumb because it works in concert with all the other fingers. The Prophet is the index finger because it is the one used to point out things. The Evangelist is the middle finger because it reaches out further than any of the others. The Pastor is the ring finger because he is married to the Church. The Teacher is the little finger because it is the only one small enough to clean out your ear. This was kind of clever and obviously memorable, but also a gross oversimplification. I have problems with several of the analogies but most of all with the one describing the Pastor as being married to the Church.

You are not married to the Church! If you *are* married, you are married to your wife. Beyond that, the Church is already spoken for. She has a man, and it is not you. She is the Bride of Christ. God does not call Pastors to be married to His Son's woman. He calls Pastors to shepherd His flock.

You may have never heard the analogy about the hand, but it is highly likely that you have heard the idea that as a Pastor your first responsibility is to God and then to the Church and everything else comes after, including your family. What you have heard is a lie designed to destroy your life's calling. I have also heard that you cannot bargain with God. That is perhaps not a lie so much as it is just wrong. (See Genesis 18:16–33.) When I was called to be a Pastor, I answered, "Yes, but…I am not going to neglect my family to lead a church." I don't know if that was a bargain or not, but I do believe God was pleased with my reply. (He likely inspired it.) I was a husband and a father before I was a Pastor. The Lord could get someone else to Pastor a church; no one else could be my wife's husband or my children's father, at least not while I was still in the picture.

The Pastor's Wife

My mother was a Pastor's daughter, a Pastor's wife, and a Pastor's mom. There has to be some sort of special crown in heaven for that kind of trifecta. Being the Pastor's wife is not about sharing the Super Trooper Spotlight, dressing in fancy clothes, and wearing flashing jewelry. That is being a show biz wife. I'm not judging those who may fit that description, but the reality for the other 99.99% of Pastors' wives is far far different.

Most Pastors are not well paid. They may only be paid a part-time salary, or may not be paid at all. This may not be a huge struggle for *the man with the call*, but it is a big deal for his household, and the person who is usually charged with running that household is his wife. God is faithful, but that doesn't mean it isn't challenging to make ends meet. Of course Pastors' wives are not the only ones who deal with this, but I just want to dispel any notion that the Pastor's home doesn't also deal with these issues. One difference between the Pastor's wife and other wives is they are often subjected to a different standard.

The Lord blessed us in that after our first child was born my wife, Margaret, was able to stay home with our children until the youngest started school. That was a period of around fourteen years. The first three of those years I was not yet in full time ministry. I was a Claims Representative for the Social Security Administration. We managed to do this by keeping careful watch on our income and spending to be sure we stayed within our budget. We also refused to go into debt except to buy a house. It is not the case with everyone, but the problem for most people who are financially stressed is on the spending side more than the lack of income side. Once you go into debt for something you *want*, it doesn't take long for the train to completely come off the rails.

Once our youngest started school, Margaret took a job as a Teacher's Aide in a Special Education Classroom. It did not pay much, but she had the same work schedule as our children's school schedule, and she was finally able to contribute to the family's income. I don't remember if she kept this job for two years or for three, but as the church grew we reached a place where we could afford to match what she was making as a Teacher's Aide. (I think it was around $6,000 a year.) We needed someone to lead the Children's Ministry, and she had already been doing that for several years on a volunteer basis, so we brought her on staff *Part Time*.

Margaret was frankly over qualified for the position. Before we met she had completed a four-year degree in Christian Education with an emphasis on Children's Ministry. She had given up her ambition of being a Children's Pastor to marry me. (This is where you see a big smile on my face.) Before our first child came she spent three years as a steel saleswoman making quite a bit more money that I was bringing in. She was clearly never afraid of work. Our church was blessed to have her. The end of the story is that she led our Children's ministry for almost thirty years before she passed away, and at her memorial service the line of people who came to honor her overflowed into the parking lot with people not just paying their respects to the family, but truly coming to honor her for what she had meant to their family.

If I was in any other line of work and my wife came to work in the *business*, it would have likely been celebrated. There can be situations where *the wife* coming to work in a situation where her husband is in charge causes problems. This is generally true where the wife has an attitude or is not really qualified for the job. But if she does the job well and actually brings positive energy to the workplace then it is a great situation. But in our case the first year that Margaret was on paid staff we had a few people leave the church because the Pastor's wife was getting paid while others were serving as volunteers. It goes without saying that none who left were people who actually contributed financially to the church.

I truly have no hard feeling toward any of the ones who left. In truth I kind of feel sorry for them. I don't think Margaret had any hard feelings either, but I share this story because this is typical of the kind of double standard Pastor's wives have to deal with. Worse than being judged by such a double standard is not letting it harden your heart. It is easy to become resentful and pick up offense. When that happens the water quickly becomes poisoned.

Money and position are not the only areas where Pastors' wives are judged by a double standard. Just about any area you can think of would fall into the same category. The clothes they wear. How their children behave. Whether or not they smile enough. In some situations they are expected to play an instrument to help lead worship. In lots of situations they are expected to lead the Women's Ministry. They are generally expected to show up for every event with their husbands and hire one of the girls in the church to baby sit. Yes, not only do most small churches largely underpay their Pastor, they also expect that they have hired a two-for-one situation with the Pastor's wife thrown in as a bonus.

None of the things I've just mentioned is the hardest thing about being a Pastor' wife. The hardest thing about being married to a Pastor falls into two main categories. First is having to, as graciously as possible, put up with hearing largely unfair criticism directed at your husband. All leaders are criticized, but it is one thing to be in a position of power, wealth, and influence while being criticized. It is quite another thing to be in a position of humility and be criticized by people who have no clue about the pressures and sacrifices required to serve the ones doing the criticizing. When I was growing up, baseball was considered the National Pastime. I'm sure it would not be labeled as such today; however, the real National Pastime is, and always has been, critical gossip.

Recently the Oscars Presentation featured Will Smith walking up on stage and physically assaulting Chris Rock for a joke he made at his wife's expense. I am quite sure that Will Smith would never have done such a thing about any joke made at his own expense, but when it came to a sensitive jab about his wife, that was an entirely different matter. Mr. Smith may have carried things too far, but I fully understand him standing up for his wife.

We all feel that way when our spouse is attacked. Pastors' wives are no different, except they can never strike back.

The second unique challenge for a Pastor's wife involves other women. The Pastor may be ugly as a stick, but there will still be other women who set their sights on him. Some have evil intent and just want to see a *man of God* fall. They may have their own personal reasons for this because of their past experiences, or they may just be that way. (I should note that it is not just women who can be *that way.*) Others look beyond any physical flaws and see the Pastor as the perfect holy man of God of whom they have always dreamed. It doesn't really occur to them that he is simply an imperfect man who scratches and makes rude noises like all men. Others simply see an authority figure, and they are attracted to authority figures. Even if the church is very small, they still feel this attraction thinking this might be an authority figure they actually have a chance to get.

The Pastor's wife isn't the only woman who may have to deal with such issues, but she is in the unique position of being handicapped in her efforts to *fight back.* Should she dress more provocatively? Better not if she's a Pastor's wife. Should she openly share displays of affection with her husband? Better not if she's a Pastor's wife. Should she confront any party who clearly has designs on her husband? Better not if she's a Pastor's wife. After all, the accused is simply a poor soul in need of guidance and spiritual comfort, and spending private time with the lonely, confused, and broken hearted is the Pastor's job, isn't it?

To protect his wife the Pastor needs to be proactive. When we first came to the church at Smyrna, we had three children ages nine months to eight years. The church also had a midweek evening service which started at 6:30. Our children's bedtime was at 7:30. For the next three years, until we had a decent nursery and children's programs at mid-week, I told my wife to stay home with the kids. Perhaps some were offended at first, but they soon got over it. If anyone complained about my wife and kids not coming to mid-week services, I simply offered them the opportunity to start a Children's Ministry for that service. No one took me up on the offer, but everyone got the message that I had boundaries when it came to my wife and family.

My wife and I agreed to never go to lunch or dinner with a member of the opposite gender alone. It didn't take us long to realize if I had to minister to a member of the opposite gender then I needed to get someone else to go with me and help *minister.* If it was during office hours, I usually left the door open, and if it needed to be closed I had a glass window installed where others could see inside.

We did two other things I highly suggest. My wife would often come up in my sermons, and when she did I always made a point to express how much I loved her and how wonderful she was. I never mentioned her in a negative light. The other thing was that we were not afraid to show affection to each other in public (including at church). It wasn't a matter of needing to *get a room,* but hugging, holding hands, and the occasional kiss were our modus operandi. At Margaret's memorial service, one of her close friends in the church shared some of the things she has learned from Margaret. One of this things was, "It is OK to kiss your husband in public."

PKs

My dad worked hard. As I have mentioned before, he was bi-vocational. Being a child there were a lot of things I didn't understand about life, but I certainly understood how I felt about my life. I resented my dad being a Pastor. I resented him not being able to work at a place where he could make a *good* living, and perhaps later on help me get such a job. I resented that it seemed all of his spare time was taken up by the needs of others in the church. I remember a specific occasion when I said to him, "You care more about everybody in the church that you do about me." (Talk about some words you'd like to have back.) I resented hearing embarrassing things about me from the pulpit. I resented the expectations others in the church and community placed on me because I was a PK. I'm sure I could think of other things I resented as well, but it's probably best I stop there. I think you get the point.

It is no wonder that PKs have a reputation for often being rebellious and perhaps even troublemakers. You can only stay penned up so long trying to meet the expectations of others before you just have to burst out of your artificial constraints to try and discover who you really are. This often involves going a little, shall we say, wild. There are all these things that you aren't allowed to see or hear or do; life experiences that most of your friends are having, and when the time comes that you have a bit of discretionary freedom… look out!

There is also the matter of God. I am thankful for the upbringing I had and how large a part God was in that upbringing; however, that was not always my attitude. As a PK you see the dark side of the church. You see the *ministers* who pass through who are far from genuine. You see the politics that often goes on in a local congregation. Plus, no matter how good your parents are, they are not perfect. You are daily under the same roof with the living embodiment of the example for the church and you notice every flaw, every inconsistency, every stumble. It often leaves you with a distaste in your mouth for *church* and perhaps even for God. In my late teens and early twenties I wanted nothing to do with the church or God for almost seven years. I am not alone in this. My story is hardly unusual.

If you grew up in the same church culture as I did there was also the annual church Business Meeting. I call it the church BM. As far as I can tell it is an almost uniquely American institution and a throw back to the book of Judges when Israel had no king and everyone did what they thought was right in their own eyes. If I seem a little bitter about the annual BM it may date back to the mid 60s. My dad had been the Pastor of Millersville First Assembly of God since 1953. He had brought the church from a dozen or so to around 120 in a community of 300. I was in my mid-teens and was totally caught by surprise when one of the more influential members of the congregation stood up in the BM and said she thought it was time for Brother Meek to go so they could bring in someone new. I may have resented my dad being a Pastor, but I also knew that he never made more than $50 a week, and I also knew somewhat of how much my dad and mom had sacrificed for this church. In retrospect this member was not mean-spirited, and she may have even been right. Nevertheless, my dad did not deserve this kind of public humiliation. It is hard to imagine a more hurtful way of handling things. For me, personally, it likely played a role in my leaving the church for so many years. I'm sure I'm far from the only PK to experience such shameful treatment of their parent(s).

A post script to the above mentioned situation. My dad was retained as the Pastor by a split vote, but the seed was planted, and within few years he was replaced.

What can you do for the PKs living in your house? It is firstly important to understand that there are no guarantees. I know that Proverbs 22:6 (NIV) says, "Start children off on the way they should go, and even when they are old they will not turn from it." Still, there are no guarantees. First of all, you may be gone before they get old and see the fruit of this advice. Even if you are still around, they have free will. Free will is why the world is a mess, but it is worth it because God thinks it is worth it and because without free will it is impossible to love. To imagine a world without free will is to imagine a world without love. I have known truly good parents whose children have not followed in their footsteps. I have known some not so good parents whose children have turned out great. Many of you are probably aware that this verse isn't so much about teaching children to be good and love God with the promise that they will eventually conform. It is about knowing your child and helping them to become what they were intended to be.

Not only is there no guarantee that your children will follow the right path, there is no one size fits all formula for the best way to raise them in the right path. Of course they need to be taught about God. It is an excellent idea to teach them the Bible. These are obvious things. The problem is really regarding *how to raise them.* Some parents are very strict and want to protect their children from *the world.* This can work well for a certain type of child, but for many, if not most, this leads to rebellion and the desire to find their own way and experience life while shutting their parents out of the process because obviously they wouldn't understand. Other parents are too lax and basically allow their children to do anything. We see this often with parents whose younger children run the household. Young children are not equip to run a household. They are not born knowing how to make decisions. They need some training and instruction.

When our children were little, their mother would never say, "What do you want for breakfast?" She also rarely said, "This is what you are having for breakfast." Instead, she would have two or perhaps three options and would say something like, "Would you like eggs or pancakes for breakfast." She was teaching them to make choices. Our oldest daughter is a great mom with two young boys. She carried on this tradition. Since the time when my wife and I were raising young children, the culture has changed. Many parents let their children basically do whatever they want, which is almost never a good idea. One of my favorite things I've heard my daughter say to her sons is, "The three-year-old does not run this house." Her's are blessed and extremely happy boys who do get to make a lot of choices as they have gotten older, but the three-year-old has never been allowed to run the house. In situations where the three-year-old *does* run the house, no one is happy, least of all the three-year-old.

One thing that a lot of parents don't seem to understand is that a teenager is not a child. Most children in our culture start seriously leaving childhood behind once they hit double digits. Of course everyone is different. Of course they will always be *your* child, but that does not at all mean they are *a* child.

When my son turned eleven, he and I spent the day together talking about life. Many parents dread *the talk*, but you really need to have it, and you really need to understand that it isn't just about, or even mainly about, sex. We talked about sex, but we also talked about life experiences. We talked about handling money. We talked about career and school choices that lay ahead. We talked about the fact that over the next ten to fifteen years we were going to disagree about some things, maybe some very important things, but that I loved him and we would come out the other side as good friends. We also talked about God. I told him that I had no doubt that he loved Jesus, but that was largely due to what his mom and I believed and that over the next ten or twenty years he would have to come to own the Faith for himself, but even if he didn't I would still love him and so would God. I also wrote him a letter telling him how proud I was of him and putting in writing some of the things we discussed. My wife had the same talk with our girls.

We brought up our kids in the Faith. We did our best to live consistent lives before them. We tried to protect them, not so much from the world, as from the church. We certainly didn't let them just watch anything, but if they were watching something questionable we watched it with them, and we would talk about it. One of the things people found weird that we didn't let them watch was *The Cosby Show*. There was no sex, language, violence, or nudity, but there was something worse in our opinion. The kids usually talked back to the parents, and not only was it presented as normal it was also funny. Rebellion isn't funny. We gave our kids a lot of freedom because we taught them how to make choices and then we let them make choices they were old enough to make. We didn't agree with all of their choices, but they knew we trusted them, and they knew they could share with us.

When we disciplined them we had three rules. Firstly, we always explained why we were disciplining them. This also guarded against us disciplining out of anger or frustration. If you are going to stop and rationally explain why you are disciplining, you will have to cool off enough to be rational. Secondly, we tried to not discipline them for simply being children. Children make childish mistakes and have simply too much energy. These things can become quite frustrating, and they may require correction, not discipline. We did; however, always discipline rebellion. Once correction is given, if it is ignored the situation has crossed over into rebellion. Thirdly, after discipline we always made sure to let the child being disciplined know that they were still greatly loved and valued.

We were blessed. The communication stayed open. None of our children went through a stage of rebellion (unless you count when they were two), and all of them have a mature solid relationship with the Lord. However, there are no guarantees.

Simply put, the best thing you can do, the most important thing you can do, really the only foundational thing you can do for your children is to love them. Love them enough to teach them and give them your time, but also love them enough to find out who they really are, not just who you want them to be. Love them in such a way that they know what love truly is and know that they are truly loved.

THE POWER OF STORIES

While attending a monthly Pastor's Meeting I heard the leader make the statement that we should only be reading non-fiction. He was saying that we should not waste our reading time on fiction. I could not let that pass. Perhaps I should have just kept quiet, but instead I raised my hand and respectfully disagreed. There are several reasons why I disagree.

What Is Truth?

Jesus stood before Pilate and told the Governor that everyone on the side of truth listens to Him. You can almost hear the sneer in Pilate's voice as he asks, "What is truth?" and then walks away not waiting for an answer. On the first day of English Class my freshman year in college, the teacher made the remark that you can always tell you are in a freshman English Class because it is the only class where you can ask "What is Truth?" and get an answer. Truth seems to be an elusive concept to many people.

There is a correct answer to the question regarding what is truth, and it is as simple and straight forward as anyone can imagine. In John 17:17 Jesus says plainly, "Your Word is truth." Ah, but not everything someone has to say about God's Word is truth. They may quote a scripture verse, and they may have some inspired revelation bringing insight into the truth, or they may quote the same scripture and then everything they have to say after is complete rubbish. Barbie Loflin is an anointed teacher of the Word at our church in Smyrna. Before she speaks she always prays, "Let all of my stuff fall to the ground and be forgotten. Let everything that is from You stand and be remembered." She is a wise woman, because virtually every speaker brings a combination of truth and "their stuff."

We have created a category of writings we call *Non-Fiction*. For many people the difference between Non-Fiction and Fiction is that Non-Fiction is true and Fiction is not true. That distinction is highly unfortunate because it is largely wrong. It would be far more accurate to say that Non-Fiction is factual, or at least it pretends to be factual, and Fiction is not factual. The difference between Truth and Facts is a significant one. Facts change. Truth doesn't change. Not all that long ago it was a medical fact that mercury was useful in curing many ailments. Today it is a fact that mercury does much harm to the body while doing almost no good. Jesus Christ rose from the dead. That's not just a fact, that is Truth.

I don't have a problem with most Non-Fiction. I enjoy a good well-researched biography. I understand that text books are basically essential for the study of most subjects. I can see great value in books that bring insight into God's Word. I do have an issue with a lot of *Christian* Non-Fiction from the late 20th century to the present. I find the Christian writers up until the mid 20th century are often of great value, but along about mid-century it became profitable to write for the Christian audience, and things changed. I'm sure there are still some good works being written about the Christian life (I can recommend virtually anything by Eugene Peterson), but there is just so much that smacks of self help and hucksterism that… well, we are drowning in it. It may be Non-Fiction but it certainly isn't Truth, and much isn't even all that factual.

I love good fiction. Fiction doesn't pretend to be factual, but it is a powerful vehicle for conveying Truth. The story is told about C.S. Lewis and his good friend J.R.R. Tolkien. Lewis came to Christ in his early thirties, and his talks with Tolkien were apparently instrumental in Lewis' conversion. One of the talks involved the nature of myth. Lewis was of a mind that much of the Bible was myth, and as such he tended to dismiss it. Tolkien brought him up short by pointing out that *myth* does not mean *untrue*.

Many Pastors, especially of the Evangelical persuasion, tend to disdain fiction as myth and therefore untrue, but they are wrong. The Bible itself proves this because much, if not most, of Jesus' teaching was in the form of parables. Just because something is called a parable doesn't mean it is sanctified fiction. It is simply fiction. It is using a non-factual story to convey Truth. If our Lord Christ used it, then I suspect it is permissible, and probably preferable, that we would also use it.

Can People Listen To Your Preaching?

In his book *Biblical Preaching* Haddon Robinson states that there are three categories of speakers. The three categories are: those you can listen to, those you cannot listen to, and those you have to listen to. Simply put, far too many Pastors fall into the category of those you cannot listen to. The main reason so many fall into this category is either because they don't know how to tell a story, or if they do they believe stories have no place in the pulpit. If they believe stories have no place in the pulpit then of course Jesus would never be invited to speak in their pulpit.

Furthermore, most people hated dry lectures in school, and they haven't warmed to them anymore just because they are in church. There is a place for reading definitions and parsing Greek verbs, but there is little place for that when you are trying to hold people's attention. There is real value in reading the great sermons of the past (some of them anyway) as a devotional exercise, but that style of preaching only had to compete with the pace of 18th and 19th century life for the attention of the listener. Today's listener is living in a world of hi def TV, twenty-four hour news, and constant social media. The message is eternal, but the methods are not.

People love stories. As soon as the speaker says, "I remember a time when…" people wake up. They perk up. People have always loved stories, and a good story teller will always hold your attention. When I was a kid I wasn't all that interested when the adults sat around talking about adult stuff, but when Steve or James started telling stories about their life and the kind of things they *got into* when they were kids, it was better than TV.

Question! Raise your hand if your favorite parts of the Bible are the genealogies. How many really get into those first ten chapters of 1 Chronicles? Raise your hand if your favorite parts of the Bible describe the division of the land in Joshua. I'm sure some people would be raising their hand right now, but I doubt it is even .01%.

Raise your hand if you really get into the laws regarding the Levitical sacrifices, the dietary laws, the rules for feasts, the rules for fasts, the rules for what to wear and how to deal with your slaves. Again, I am sure there are some raised hands, especially about the dietary laws, but not that many. Of course, this is in no way a scientific study, but I'm going to be generous and say we are up to 10%.

Raise your hand if your favorite parts of the Bible are the Books of Wisdom. The poetry and the proverbs are quite attractive to a lot of people. I would add much of Isaiah to that category because of the powerful poetry the prophet uses. I may be underestimating here but let's give this 15% of the hands raised.

What's left? Predictive prophesy is attractive to a lot of people; however, I personally consider it to be essentially an outlier. It is a topic that can generate a lot of excitement, but that level of interest burns like a match, not a candle. The excitement is usually generated by fairly wild speculation, and we never seem to learn that there is little value in such speculation. I'm not just referring to the countless failed predictions about the Second Coming. (I believe He is coming back, but I also believe no one knows the time of His coming except the Father.) We should also consider the situation regarding Christ's first coming as a cautionary tale. Those who were deep into studying the prophecies about the coming Messiah were the most likely to not recognize Jesus because of their preconceived notions that arose from those studies. We think we have more wisdom than they did. We don't. I'll give maybe 1% to those who not only get into predictive prophesy but also stay into it as their favorite study.

We are up to 26.01%. Whatever could the other 73.99% claim as their favorite part of the Bible? You guessed it. Stories. You may call it History if you prefer, but history is, in fact, stories. Without stories there is no history. Stories are the container that allows history to exist. Cain killed his brother and was cursed. Abraham trusted God and was blessed. Jacob deceived his father Isaac and was himself deceived by his sons regarding what happened to Joseph. Joseph was sold into slavery by his brothers, but God used that to bring about the creation of the nation of Israel. Moses led Israel through the Red Sea. Joshua commanded the Sun and Moon to stand still. David killed Goliath. David had Uriah killed. Isaiah saw the Lord high and lifted up. Jonah was swallowed by a great fish. Jesus died on the cross for our sin and then rose from the dead. Stories and stories and stories. Carriers of Truth. If three quarters of the people (or more) are the most interested in stories then why aren't we telling stories in the pulpit?

Far too many Pastors are not good story tellers. How in the world can seminaries claim to train Pastors without offering extensive training in story telling?

Fortunately almost anyone can learn to be a good story teller. How? Read good fiction. When I say *good* fiction I am not talking about a moral judgment. I am talking about writers who are able to tell stories that cause you to stay up way past your bedtime turning page after page. Some people sneer at the notion of fiction saying it is *unreality*. Why? Unreality simply means it takes us to a place or time we can't actually visit in this world. It takes us to a place and time we cannot see with our literal eyes. It takes us to a place and time we can only visit in the spirit. It takes us to a place of heroes and valor and beauty far beyond what exist in the fallen world which we currently inhabit. Why is this a bad thing? Why do we consider this of little value?

The Bible says, "Eye has not seen, ear has not heard, neither has it entered into the mind of man the things that God has prepared for those who love Him." The Bible also says, "We fix our eyes not on what is seen, but on what is unseen. What is seen is temporary, but what is unseen is eternal." What we think of as being "real" is actually just a whiff of smoke that is passing away. The Real is on the other side of the veil. If all you can see is what you see with your eyes then you can listen to all the teaching in this world about faith but you will never learn to live by faith.

Why did God choose Jacob instead of Esau? Jacob was the kind of guy who always seemed to have an angle. He would take advantage of you and even stab you in the back (metaphorically) if he got the chance. Esau was not only the first born, he was seemingly generous, a lot of fun (his dad's favorite), and while he might be quick to anger he was also quick to forgive. Why did God choose Jacob? Esau was the kind of guy who when choosing between a bowl of stew which he could see and a birthright which was invisible, chose the stew. Jacob was the kind of guy who had a faith that could reach beyond the visible, could reach beyond *reality*, and see the value of the invisible. Without faith it is impossible to please God.

If Pastors who need to become better story tellers would just read good fiction they could learn to tell stories that hold the attention of their listeners. They could learn to use metaphors that drive home the point and images that stick in the mind. Instead, they don't read fiction because they consider it to be a waste of time. Consequently, many of their listeners consider their sermons to be a waste of time.

The Word Of Our Testimony

In the fall of 1975, I visited The Lord's Chapel for the first time. The Chapel was a church across town that was making news because it was basically the forefront of the Charismatic Renewal in the Nashville area. It was also being led by a man with whom I had been acquainted since my childhood. I had never really heard him preach, but I had always liked him and was eager to hear him. When I got to the service I was disappointed to learn that he wasn't going to be there that evening, and the new Youth Pastor would be speaking. When Mike Nelson got up to speak I was still feeling some disappointment. Five minutes later I was no longer disappointed. Within the next thirty minutes I was transformed.

Over the years I have named Mike many times as my favorite preacher to listen to. I'm hardly alone in this opinion. Mike passed away in 2003, but those who got to hear him remember a man who was immanently relatable. He seemed to be speaking directly to every person in the room. You felt as if you knew him. He would usually teach for forty minutes or so, but regardless of how long he went, when he finished you always felt it was too soon. How did he weave this magic? He told stories. Most of his stories were about his life.

Having grown up in the church as a PK, I had heard well over a thousand sermons from scores of Pastors, evangelists, and missionaries. I said that hearing Mike for the first time was transformative, and that is not too strong a word. I had never heard anyone bring the Word like this. He was *real*. He was transparent. He was genuine. And his stories were great. Had I never run into Mike Nelson, or someone like him, I doubt I would have ever had the desire to enter the pulpit. When I *did* start teaching the Word, I was at first worried that maybe I was trying to be like Mike until I realized that even if I was trying to be like Mike it would come out like me, not Mike. The reason was because I wasn't telling Mike's stories, I was telling mine, and they were interesting.

90

The Bible says we overcome the devil by the blood of the Lamb and the word of our testimony. Have you ever heard a really great testimony? Are you both inspired and intimidated by such a testimony? Don't be. Perhaps you have never been in prison, or a drug addict, or seriously injured in war, or delivered from mob connections, or miraculously healed, etc, etc, etc. Those are fascinating stories, but so is yours. The fact is that many people simply cannot relate to the speaker with the *wow!* testimony. What they can relate to is someone who has had a *normal* life dealing with the same kind of issues they face and who over a period of ordinary days has come to find Jesus to be real on a day to day level.

In the early 1980s my wife and I led a home Bible study. It was mostly attended by folks in their twenties and thirties. One of the guys was a new convert named Lee. Lee had asked the Lord to show him someone who was like him, about the same age and similar circumstances, who was seriously following Jesus. He met Harry in our Bible study and immediately knew that God had answered his prayer, so he decided to start seriously following Jesus. You may think there is nothing *special* about your testimony, your stories. You may be right, but understand that your *ordinary* testimony is exactly what some people are looking for to encourage them to follow Jesus.

Everyone has a story. Many years after I graduated from University, I visited one of my old professors. He told me about going to the 60th reunion of his high school class. He dreaded going to it. He was from a small town and had not had any contact with the few members of his class since graduation. He described walking into a room full of strangers. They had a dinner and afterward that which he dreaded came upon him. Someone said, "Let's go around the table and everyone share about what has been going on in their life."

He certainly had things to share. He graduated from the Naval Academy at Annapolis. He had served as a submarine Captain. He was now the Dean of Arts and Sciences at a large University.

It turns out there were a surprising number of remarkable stories shared as they went around the table. Finally they came to the last one. This lady started out by saying that she had never really been anywhere having lived her entire life in this small Middle Tennessee town. She had not gone on to earn any degrees. She had just been a wife and mother with nine children. At that point everyone's ears perked up, but she wasn't finished. I don't remember the exact details, but it turns out that of those nine children at least three were medical doctors and two were University Presidents. She truly did not think her story was very interesting, but by the time she finished sharing there wasn't a dry eye in the room.

Everyone has a story, and their story is their testimony. When I was growing up there were two words that in retrospect I now know were seriously abused. Those words were "Story" and "Testimony." Story was often used as a synonym for lie. I can still hear my mom saying, "Ronnie, are you telling me a story?" Testimony was limited to telling how you came to Jesus, or perhaps occasionally expanded to include some perhaps miraculous event in your life. I think we have established that *story* is to *lie* as *fruit* is to *orange*. A story may be a lie, but it certainly doesn't have to be anymore than a fruit has to be an orange. Furthermore, just because something claims to be factual doesn't guarantee that you aren't being told a lie.

Testimony isn't just about *some* of your life, it is about *all* of your life. You don't have to have a headline grabbing event to have a testimony. You don't have to have major motion picture potential in your history to have a story that relates. Ninety-nine percent of your listeners don't have this kind of story. These have the kind of story you have, and if you will share your story you will connect with them in such a way that they will be open to seeing how God is part of every facet of their day 24/7/365. As you connect with them and their lives the Bible will come alive. It will no longer be stained glass figures living disconnected lives that we cannot be a part of, but living breathing flesh and blood humans who in the course of the ordinary encounter the eternal. If you will share your stories they will be inspired to share their stories, and testimony will happen.

If you will become real, the stories in the Bible will become real. When the stories in the Bible become real, God becomes real.

CREDIBILITY

My friend Eddie Turner refers to credibility as "having enough change in your pocket" to get something done. Credibility is a major asset for any leader, but this is especially the case for a Pastor. Other leaders may have the ability to promote their followers or increase their pay, but Pastors do not really have these options. This is not a bad thing. Jesus said that the leaders of the Gentiles "lord it over" those under them, but it is not to be that way with us. If people are going to follow you as their Pastor they need to know you are genuine. You need to have credibility.

Let's be clear about one thing, your authority does not come from your credibility with the people. If you get this confused you will end up attempting to please people rather than pleasing God. You will fall into the trap of Saul's second fear mentioned earlier. You will be following the people instead of them following you, and neither of you will be following God. All true authority comes from God, and there will be times when, in order for you to follow God's leading, you will have to go in a direction that people do not understand. This is when credibility comes strongly into play. Your credibility is really for the benefit of the people, not yourself.

Read that last sentence again.

It is far too easy to abuse credibility for one's own purposes. You want something but encounter resistance. You can do the hard work required to understand the resistance and reach an outcome that works for all involved, or you can spend some of that change in your pocket to bull your way to silencing any opposition. If you choose the second of these routes one of two things will happen. Either you will soon find yourself with essentially no one following you, or you will create an organization that may glorify you, but it will only pretend to glorify God. You may say it glorifies God, but that will only be because you have your own identity confused with the Deity.

If you understand that your credibility is for the good of the people then you will only use it when the need arises to move in a direction that God has clearly laid out but that others may not understand. Do not use it frivolously. If you are simply using it because you are too frustrated to explain something, or because you are getting push back in a questionable matter then it will not take long for you to discover that your pocket is empty when you really need some of that change.

Credibility comes with time. You may have a season where you have some signs that appear to be miraculous (they may even *be* miraculous) which will give you something called *instant credibility*, but the kind of people who will follow you for that reason will also follow the next guy who comes along doing *stuff.* The kind of credibility that will count with solid people who you can count on is earned over time. They need to know they can count on you. They aren't looking for someone who is always right—they know better than to look for that. They are looking for someone they can trust to shoot straight with them and be honest. They are looking for someone with whom they can trust their money, their time, their families, and their lives.

Earlier I mentioned Mike Nelson and what a wonderful speaker he was. He was the Youth Pastor at The Lord's Chapel, and because he was such a wonderful speaker, he was a teen magnet. The average attendance at Youth meetings was seventy-five. I know that today's mega churches have much larger groups, but in the 1970s that was a large youth group. Mike left the Chapel in 1977 to start a new church on the other side of Nashville. He was replaced as Youth Pastor by Bruce Coble.

Bruce Coble is a close friend who became an instrumental figure in my life. There are certain people the Lord connects you with and as the years pass, regardless of what different paths you may take, it seems that He keeps you connected in such a way that He obviously intends for you to be a significant person in each other's walk. Bruce was one of those people. The Lord has kept us bonded through several different churches and over two different continents for a period of over forty years.

Bruce took over from Mike Nelson. In some ways Bruce and Mike were almost polar opposites but could work well together. For several years Bruce worked with Mike in the Youth Group. Mike would teach, and Bruce would sit along the back wall with the guys who were *less interested* in the spiritual side of things. At first I was puzzled by this, because I'm the kind who thinks you set the example by being engaged yourself with what is going on, and that didn't seem to be what Bruce was doing. I later discovered that Bruce was certainly engaged, but he sat back with these guys because his presence brought a level of focus and stability to a group that was otherwise lacking in those attributes.

I will never forget the first youth meeting which Bruce led. Mike was a dynamic engaging speaker. Bruce was a good teacher, but no one would ever accuse him of being dynamic. In fact it seemed that his goal was to be sort of anti-dynamic. (Of course this is biblical. "I must decrease so He can increase.") I no longer remember the exact passage Bruce chose for that first meeting, but I do remember that it was a rather obscure couple of verses from one of the Minor Prophets. Listening to Mike had been like eating ice cream. Listening to Bruce that night was like eating Brussels sprouts. The result of this fairly drastic change was easily predictable. The meeting size shrank quickly. As the high school cheerleaders started to disappear so did the group of guys siting along the back wall. Mike left in the autumn. By the start of winter we reached a low of eight in attendance.

Over the next six months something happened. By the end of summer our youth group started averaging seventy-five again. What was it? Did Bruce find his teen magnet speaking mojo? No, though I don't recall any more sermons from the minor prophets (unless it was Jonah). What happened was that Bruce would tell the kids that we were going to do a cookout, or a service project, or a night of racquetball. Bruce would tell the kids this was going to happen, and without fail it happened. Mike was a great speaker but he wasn't always the best on his follow through. (We all have our gifts and our weaknesses.) When Bruce planned something for the kids, it didn't matter if five or fifty showed up, it happened. The kids learned that they could trust Bruce. He had gained credibility, and as a result he had almost five years of fruitful youth ministry that has impacted the world for decades and generations. (I won't go into the stories, but what I just said about the fruitfulness of his ministry is no exaggeration.) If you are unimpressed by a mere five years of youth ministry in one place then you are woefully ignorant of the average tenure of most Youth Pastors.

How To Get Credibility

(Honesty + Humility + Faithfulness) X Time = Credibility.

Instant credibility is usually instantly lost. The formula shown above is the only real way to achieve genuine credibility. There are no shortcuts. Some people claim credibility by pointing to their results, but this is a bogus metric. Those who point to such results are using a worldly standard. God could care less about the world's measurements. They might be evidence that one is an Eliab, but they will never tell you anything about who is a David—a man or woman after God's own heart. Had Bruce's Youth Group stayed at a small handful they would have still impacted the world for

Christ. It wasn't how many Bruce had following him that mattered, but the fact that Bruce was setting an example of honestly, humbly, and faithfully following Christ that made the difference.

How To Keep Credibility

Credibility is hard to get and easy to lose. There are several simple things that will help you keep credibility. Be as honest as you can be, speaking the truth in love. Be humble enough to admit when you are wrong and understand that this will at times require you needing to apologize to others. Be consistent (faithful). I tell parents something that is sorely lacking in today's parenting methods. Never threaten your child but do warn them. The difference between a threat and a warning is that a threat is simply an attempt to manipulate your child by means of empty words. A warning is used to help your child avoid an unpleasant experience. It takes little time for a child to learn when their parents are simply making threats. If you don't follow through and you aren't consistent, you are toast. In a similar manner, as a leader, if you are not consistent people will pick up on that in short order, and once they do your credibility is done.

I believe the single most important thing you can have to help you be honest, humble, and consistent is people around you who will tell you the truth. Bullies may look like leaders at times, but in truth they are simply bullies, and by definition a bully is a scared big boy or girl. A bully cannot be a godly leader. They may Pastor a church, perhaps even a large church, but they cannot be a godly leader, because their mode of operation is intimidation used to manipulate others. God does not use these methods.

No one likes to think of themselves as being a bully, but there is a simple test to determine if one is a bully or not. Do you have people around you who will tell you the things you may not want to hear? If your *inner circle* is only filled with people who always agree with you then you may be pretty certain that you are a bully.

All leaders need an inner circle. Even Jesus had one. A healthy inner circle will be composed of people who are united in heart but do not necessarily share the same perspective. It is true that a small group that shares the same perspective can do mighty things, they just aren't likely to be doing them for the Kingdom of God. They may be doing them for a church or for a particular idea or bias but ultimately you discover that while all of this *advancement* may be for a church or a particular idea, or perhaps even a lead personality, it is of little or no value for God's Kingdom.

There were two dear men with whom I shared many years of fruitful ministry. One was Bruce Coble and the other was a worship Pastor named Wayne Berry. Our families have been connected for over forty years, and we all served on the staff together at the church in Smyrna, Tennessee, for over twenty years. We shared a common love for Jesus and a desire to truly follow Him. We had similar ideas about how to lead a church and disciple others; however, there were many areas about which we disagreed. Furthermore, there were times when we would get quite upset with one another. In other words, we were a great gift from God in each other's lives. The areas about which we disagreed were non-essential areas. Being confronted about your ideas in non-essential areas by people you love and trust is a great blessing, and if you are willing and secure enough to have such relationships you will find that credibility will almost certainly be the result.

Tithes and Giving

There are different camps within the Christian community regarding the issue of tithes. There is really no reason for me to go over the arguments pro and con for whether or not we are required to tithe because doing so is not likely to change anyone's mind. I will simply state what I believe. I believe that tithing is biblical and not something that passed away at some point in the past. I believe that while tithing is not a factor in our salvation it is an important component of discipleship, especially in a consumer culture. I do not judge nor condemn those who do not tithe, but I believe they are missing out on a great blessing. I also believe that there is quite a bit of room for discussion about *where* the tithe should go.

One of the greatest blessings of my upbringing was being taught to tithe. If I had a dime I gave a penny. If I had a dollar I gave ten cents. If I had a quarter I would round up and give three cents. We have a family in the church at Smyrna whose teenaged children would give an amount along the lines of $73.47. This would show up on the quarterly report I reviewed, and it said to me that these kids were being taught to tithe. The reason I consider it a great blessing to have been taught to tithe as a child is because when I became an adult believer, even after a seven year period as a prodigal, whether or not to tithe was never an issue. Whenever I made any money the first thing I did was set aside the ten percent I was going to give to the Lord.

I can testify that the blessings I have seen are obvious. My parents were the example. My dad had an eighth grade education. He was a bi-vocational Pastor who also sold shoes retail and occasionally worked as a butcher. My mom taught public school in a lower income county. She started in the mid 1950s making $150 a month. We weren't dirt poor, but we did have to gather manna on a daily basis, metaphorically speaking. There was no financial inheritance that either of them ever received and no great investment opportunity of which they took advantage. Yet, they managed to retire wanting for nothing. They owned a house. They never missed a meal. They could afford to do a little traveling and each month they had a little more coming in with Social Security and mom's teacher retirement than they had going out. Yes, they tithed on everything they made both during their working and retirement years.

Tithing isn't just about getting financial blessings. I learned that when I tithe God takes care of things. When I don't tithe then I am responsible for making ends meet, but when I put God first

He is the one responsible. There is great peace in that situation. Romans 11:16 says,

If the part of the dough offered as firstfruits is holy, then the whole batch is holy; if the root is holy, so are the branches. (NIV) If I take the first ten percent and give it to the Lord then I understand that the other ninety percent is also holy to the Lord. This totally impacts the way I look at the money He has entrusted to me. I no longer see it as my money, but His money. This frees me to be generous but also wise.

It is easy and fun to be generous with someone else's money. This is especially true if that someone else has limitless resources. After I have tithed, if God wants me to give somewhere else I'm attuned to listening to Him, because I already have established that this is His, not mine. Indeed, it is more blessed to give than receive. This is true not just because you have the means to give rather than being in a situation where you need to receive, but also because it is just freaking fun to give. If you have ever bought a special present or been able to provide for someone else's need then you know the joy and excitement that comes with such giving. There have been times in my life when I have made investment choices that I later deeply regretted. I have never regretted anything that I have given away, except for the times I wish I had given more.

Establishing the fact that all of the money belongs to God will also make you wise in what you do with the other ninety percent. I am subject to the occasional impulse purchase, but the key word is *occasional*. More importantly, if there is a large item that I really want, literally the Spirit of God constrains me. Am I going to go into debt for this thing and use God's money to service that debt? The only time this makes sense is if the thing in question is going to appreciate in value. Real estate is about the only thing that generally meets this criteria. Otherwise, if I don't want this thing enough to wait until I can pay cash that is a strong indication that buying it is a truly bad idea.

Some people may be almost offended by me saying the Spirit of

God constrains me when it comes to spending, but they shouldn't be. If I truly consider the money to belong to God then I truly believe He is interested in how it is spent. If I truly believe the Holy Spirit lives within me then that is a 24/7 proposition, and He is interested in every area of my life. Whenever I walk into a situation when I am likely to purchase something I breathe this simple prayer; "Help me to buy what I should buy and not buy what I should not buy." By the way, I'm by no means a miser. I do spend. I just ask for His help.

When you do give, either to the Church or to others, you really need to develop a short memory. In giving to my church I am actually giving to the Lord. My giving doesn't buy me a seat at the decision table. I have not earned extra points with God by tithing. If I think otherwise then I might as well not give. When I give to help someone else there is that initial joy of giving, but then it's time to move on. The person receiving doesn't owe me anything, or it wasn't really a gift. God doesn't really owe me anything for being generous with His money.

Teaching Tithing

When I came to the church in Smyrna I was conflicted about teaching tithing. Ever since Oral Roberts started hiring professional fund raisers to design mail out campaigns and Jim Bakker started crying on TV about having to shut down the program if more money didn't start coming in the topic of money has become a complicated issue in the Church. On the one extreme you have those who have made money the major topic. They *teach* about tithing and giving as if it were some sort of investment opportunity. *Plant your seed faith here, and if you put in X amount of dollars then you can expect 30X, 60X, or even 100X in return.* On the other extreme are those who just simply don't talk about it at all. The baskets are in the back, and if you happen to find one and want to give something then fine, if not then fine, we don't really care and neither does God. In fact, God cares quite a bit about what we do with our money.

When I came back to the Lord in the 1970s I attended a church on the second extreme mentioned above. It was so refreshing. It was as if all of the Christian hucksters on TV didn't exist. When I came to Smyrna in the late 1980s we didn't go so far as to not make offering time a part of the service, but I avoided saying much about it for the first few years, because I did not want to be classified with the *Seed Faith* gang or with the *begging for dollars* gang. As is often the case, going to either extreme is not the solution. The cure to bad teaching about money isn't no teaching about money. What needs to happen is good teaching about money.

Money is a powerful thing, not because of what it can buy but because of the spirit connected to it. Money is itself inanimate, but the spirit connected to money is quite active. Either you will control your money or your money will control you. This is not a *maybe*. This is a certainty. We live in a capitalistic, consumer culture. We are constantly bombarded by influences urging us to consume, to buy. We are constantly being told that we *deserve* to have bigger and better. We are constantly being assured that if we just had one of these or more of that we would be healthier, more attractive, happier, and an all around better person. The key to this better life is money.

In contrast, the Bible teaches us that the key to a better life, an abundant life, eternal life, is God Himself. God's chief rival for our affection isn't some foreign deity or some ancient pagan deity. His chief rival is money. I teach tithing and giving, but not as a means to get more money. I teach it as a means of putting money in its proper place and getting more of God. This isn't a matter of buying God. All that God is and has is free and available. The more we follow in discipleship and invite Him into every area of our lives the more of God we have. I look at tithing and how we handle our money as a barometer of where our relationship with God stands. I'm not the only one. Jesus said, "Where your treasure is, there your heart is also." If He were speaking in today's vernacular He might well have said, "Show me your check book and I'll show you what you love the most."

As a Pastor charged with feeding the flock, I have come to understand that if I am not intentionally seeing that the flock gets sound teaching about money then I am leaving an important part of my job undone. Don't be intimidated into silence by all of the bad teaching that has brought disrepute to the cause of Christ. Teach what is true, what is good, and what is helpful in bringing your people to follow Christ. I believe tithing is foundational in that teaching, but even if you do not agree that tithing is for us today you should teach that faithful giving and generosity is a keynote in the truly Christ-centered life.

Numbers

"We count people because people count." I've heard it several times, and occasionally I actually believed it; however, it is really a matter of motive. I believe that often times we count people because the bank requires us to. Sometimes we count people to gauge whether or not we are *succeeding* as a Pastor. If the numbers are trending in the right direction, we may even count people to feel good about ourselves. I grew up with a Numbers Board on the wall of our sanctuary. It was a far simpler time, and someone would hand change the numbers each week telling us how many were in attendance and what the attendance had been the same week last year. If we had 124 instead of last year's 121, we felt good. If the numbers were reversed, we didn't feel good. None of it really had anything to do with God.

Moses did count the people because God told him to do so. David once counted the people, and it was very displeasing to God. The difference between these two situations was a matter of the heart and of trust in God. If a Pastor feels they need to know the numbers on a frequent basis, I fear they have their eyes on the wrong thing. One can excuse this as being a good steward or needing to plan for the future of the church, but I find that highly suspect. The future of the church should be a matter of hearing from God, not some man-made five year plan. Can God give us a five year plan? Yes, but He doesn't usually bring us into the know too far in advance because if we think we know where we are going we will try to get there under our own steam. The *Five Year Plan* idea did not come from the Bible but from Business School.

I do agree that we need to know the condition of the flock, and the numbers can tell us some things, but becoming obsessed with the numbers is a seriously dangerous situation. I'm not at all claiming to be perfect in this, but here is what I did.

Regarding Attendance

Our business manager would send out monthly general numbers, and I would read them, but I didn't let them influence me too much. First of all I tried not to let them influence me regarding myself. If the numbers are great, we tend to feel good about ourselves and think that means we are for sure doing it right for the Lord. Of course this doesn't necessarily mean that at all. I'm sure Saul was quite popular with the people after his defeat of the Amalekites. He won a great victory. He let the people have their way. He even got a monument to himself out of the deal. He was not so popular with God. In fact, he was disobedient and lost his kingdom even though he was at the height of his popularity. On the other hand, after saving the city of Keilah, the people of that city turned on David and were willing to hand him over to Saul. Jeremiah was never popular. Jesus had thousands leave Him after hearing His teaching. Numbers do not tell you where you stand with God.

Numbers also do not tell you what you should do next. If you are going to build a new building, or open a new campus, or plant a new church it should be because God told you to and not because of the numbers. The flip side is also true. For years we had an early service. It wasn't a different worship style. It wasn't a different teaching. It wasn't well attended. I didn't start this service because we needed more room. I started it, and continued with it for over twenty years, because I believed that was what God told me to do. Was I right? I don't know, but if you believe God has told you to do something and you don't do it, what does that say?

Regarding Finances

As the Senior Pastor I was the Chairman of the Administrative Board at our church. We were an Elder-ruled church, but I had discovered that just because a person had a call as an Elder did not mean that they also had the gift of administration. Furthermore, if the Elders were directly overseeing the church finances, those issues tended to take up all of the time in our Elder's meetings leaving little time for the spiritual matters of the church which the Elders should be addressing. Our solution was for the Elders to appoint an Administrative Board made up of members selected and approved by the Elders. In the case of some truly big decisions, such as building a new facility, The Elders would get directly involved with the Admin Board, but with all other matters—What to do about the broken AC unit? Who to hire to repave the parking lot? What should be in the new annual budget?—the Admin Board made the decisions.

I was the Chairman of the Board, but I did not try to become too involved with most of the decisions. I was there to conduct the meeting, and if they asked my advice about priorities I was able to give them my opinion first hand. It worked quite well for us. Regarding staff salaries I would occasionally have a suggestion concerning someone on staff. In over a decade this may have happened two or three times when I thought someone was being overlooked. I never really gave input regarding my salary. I excused myself for the main discussion and vote on salaries. This also worked quite well for us.

For the first several years I intentionally did not even look at the giving records. Then the Lord convicted me about this being a part of my job. The last couple of decades I was at the church I would receive a quarterly report about individual giving. There were of course some surprises. I started to see things I had not seen before, and I genuinely felt like this was a part of knowing the condition of the flock.

The reason I had not been looking at these numbers was to not be unduly influenced by how much individuals gave. Once I started looking at the numbers the undue influence turned out to not be an issue. What I did see was a glimpse into various lives. My heart would be deeply touch by seeing the faithfulness of some who I knew had little. Other times I was made aware of those who were experiencing struggles. This was indicated by a sharp drop off in their contributions. Sometimes these struggles were with the church itself. It didn't cause me to automatically reach out to them, but it did put them on my radar to ask the Lord what was going on and if I should reach out to the individual. Other times the struggles involved reversals in their financial situation. In these cases I would be more likely to reach out to them to see if they were in need of some assistance.

What I did not do was keep weekly tabs on either attendance or individual giving. Weekly numbers don't really tell you anything useful. Here is a valuable piece of info: weeks are going to fluctuate. If giving is down there is needless worry. You may call it *concern* if you like. If giving is up that feels good, but just understand that it may be down the next week. These are distractions that create the mostly false notion that God is speaking to us through the numbers. When it comes to attendance remember Gideon. The numbers were encouraging, but the Lord said, "You have too many for Me to use you to defeat the enemy." Numbers do not tell the real story.

If you may be thinking that you are immune to the emotional swings caused by following the weekly numbers, I would simply asks you to remember how you usually feel on Easter. Now, remember how you feel the week after Easter.

I'll close this section with the story my friend Dave shared with me. Dave was leading a growing church and there was high excitement come Easter Sunday. (I prefer to call it Resurrection Sunday, but I don't have the problem with the word *Easter* that some have.) Easter came, and there was a good crowd for the service. More importantly, Dave's stepdaughter, who was in a prodigal period of rebellion and running from the Lord, responded to the altar call and made a fresh, and ultimately lasting, commitment to the Lord at that service. Everything was wonderful until Dave looked at the numbers that afternoon. It was a large crowd but it was fewer than last Easter. Dave was somewhat bummed out. The Lord rebuked Dave in no uncertain terms. He clearly heard the Lord say, "Your daughter came home to the faith today, and you are downcast about the service because of the number of people who were present. What is wrong with you?"

I think we can all agree that it is best to see things through God's eyes. American success stories are all about numbers. God success stories rarely have anything to do with numbers.

PART 3
WHAT'S NEXT?

Transition

We have established the fact that your ministry will not last forever. Some day there will hopefully be another who will take your place. Unless you simply die unexpectedly, there should be an opportunity for a prepared transition. If you come from a tradition that believes in something called Apostolic Succession then transition is pretty much out of your hands, but those who come from other traditions generally have some input to help prepare for the hand-off of leadership. This is an important period for the church and for your ministry. Most people are quite uncomfortable with change, but if it is done right it can be a fruitful time.

Jesus put a good deal of effort into preparing His followers for transition. He told them that He was going away. He told them why He was going away. He told them some of the mistakes they were going to make and what to expect from the world after He was gone. He assured them it was going to be alright and explained that His going was actually going to be better than having Him stay with them. He even prepared leaders to step in and lead after He was gone. If Jesus felt the need to do this then surely it should be on our *to do* list as well.

David did not do such a great job of transition. He knew who the next king was supposed to be. He had told Bathsheba and the prophet Nathan that the next king was to be Solomon. He neglected to inform his sons of this decision. He also did not inform the influential leaders in Israel. In short, he knew, but he didn't prepare. As a result Adonijah, Solomon's older brother, recruited some influential leaders as allies and had himself anointed as king. Everyone knew that David's time was near, and there had been no clear instructions, so Adonijah took matters into his own hands.

You can read the story in 1 Kings 1. (Hopefully you already know it.) This situation caused a great deal of confusion in the country. It created a situation where Solomon came to the throne with ready-made internal enemies which caused him to ultimately have to execute some who could have been valuable allies because the conspiracy to make Adonijah king was still bubbling under the surface. Solomon did become king, but his ascension to the throne was unnecessarily hard and complicated by David's lack of preparation.

When Is It Time?

Being an American I come from a church culture where it is sort of a badge of honor to put in long hours and ultimately *Burn Out for Christ.* For some this means you know when it is time because you are watching your funeral service from the other side. It's not that drastic for everyone. Some will consider retirement when they can no longer walk. I am being a little facetious here, but there is too much truth in what I'm saying. The point is that if you are waiting for your body to tell you when to retire then you are listening to the wrong voice. Jesus asks us to take up our cross, but He does not ask us to *Burn Out.* That tends to be our own idea; one we got from the culture around us.

When I retired at the age of 71, it was not because I was tired, though I did discover after I retired that I really was tired. Taking a break for a few months was greatly refreshing, and there seems to still be quite a bit of tread left on the tires. That does not mean that I retired too early. It means that it was simply time for a new chapter in my life. It was also time for a new chapter in our church's life. The church needed a younger perspective. It needed a Senior Pastor with more energy and fresh vision. When the new guy came on, he did not do everything the way I would do it. If he did everything the way I would do it there would have been no point in him coming on.

If you have children of a certain age you have almost certainly experienced the moment when you made a reference to some well known artist, hero, athlete, or event of importance to you, and your child looked at you like you were speaking in tongues. "Who? What?" It happens without us even thinking about it. Time passes. In the words of Paul, "Every generation throws a hero up the pop charts." (Not Saint Paul, or Paul McCartney, but Paul Simon. "You know, Simon and Garfu... ah, never mind.")

I did not retire because I was tired. I did not retire because most of the people in our church no longer knew who Chubby Checker was. (Google it.) I retired because God told me it was time. If you retire for any other reason then you are retiring for the wrong reason. Many Pastors hold on too long. Their identity is tied up in being a Pastor. They have been at the same church so long they start to think of it as *their church* and can't really see it under the leadership of someone who might change things. They may even hold off retirement for financial reasons as they are afraid they won't have the income they need once they step down. These things are the world's way of doing business. The Kingdom way of doing business is to listen to God.

How Do You Prepare?

I mentioned in the previous chapter that God would likely send you younger leaders for you to prepare for leadership. I know that in many traditions the Pastor is selected by an authority outside the church and that it is almost a given that the new Pastor will come from outside the local church. It is God's church, and He can do what He wants to do. I am not in a position to judge others; however, I think it is a healthy and spiritually organic situation for the next Pastor to come from within the local church. The Pastor's job is largely accomplished through relationships, and it takes more than a few months or even a few years to create those relationships. Much of what I am going to say about preparing for transition is not going to apply to many situations, but if you are in a position where the local leadership has the authority and the willingness to consider selecting a new Pastor from within, I will share what I have learned. If you are not in such a situation you still have the responsibility to prepare the young leaders God has sent to you for their service both in their church and elsewhere.

The first thing is to identify the potential leaders. You will certainly need God's help in this. Ultimately the Holy Spirit makes the call, but in terms of what to look for, I would place a sincere desire to follow Jesus at the top of the list. Not everyone who wants to follow Jesus is supposed to be a leader in the church, but every leader in the church must have this sincere desire. Next, looking for the leadership traits is pretty obvious. Does this person tend to lead? Do others tend to follow this person? Once you have identified these people, you simply need to be intentional about pouring into their lives in some way. This may involve one-on-one time or perhaps group sessions.

At our church I identified a group of six or eight young leaders and invited them to a once a month group session. We got to know each other and for several months I did a teaching on leadership. In addition to Bible study, we went through different books that had been especially helpful in my life. We looked at our own church to help see it through each others eyes. I usually did the majority of the talking, but that was not the case every month. I encouraged discussion and questions. I wanted to hear them express themselves equally as much as I wanted them to hear me. When a question would come up, the goal was to arrive at an answer, or more likely an understanding, together.

I started intentionally doing this around five years before I actually retired, though I was doing it informally for several years prior. Over the years the group changed. Some dropped out. Others joined. Some ended up going to other churches, hopefully the better for having been a part of our group. Most stayed at our church and are currently in leadership positions, both volunteer and on staff.

Preparing Others

The most important thing, in fact the only thing that truly matters, is choosing the person God has chosen. If this is really God's choice then having opposition will just be something you have to deal with and God will sort it out. If this is not God's choice then it doesn't matter how enthusiastic the people are—there will be no real fruit. This being understood I think it is important for the Pastor to lead the transition by communicating clearly and attempting to bring the people into unity behind the new Pastor.

Our church has an Elder Ruled polity. It was important to have the Elders genuinely on board with the new Pastor. If you have been involved with an Eldership you understand what I mean by "genuinely on board." If you are paying attention to your flock, you know the difference between people saying they are on board and them actually being on board. Don't let yourself be fooled by what you want others to think. It isn't enough to have your Elders or Church Board in a position where the majority of members are 55% on board or even 60% on board. We aren't talking about a unanimous group that is 100% on board. That would likely not be a real thing anyway. I would say having the least enthused one being at least 75% on board would give the new Pastor a solid base from which to work. You may not be able to get that, but with God's help you can try.

Since we are Elder Ruled I did all of the ground work with that group before bringing anything to the congregation. I believe it is a big part of the job of the Elders to protect the congregation from division. When divisive issues get into the larger body there will of course be differing opinions. Differing opinions isn't the problem. The problem is that there will also be a fair amount of spiritual immaturity dealing with those differing opinions. The next thing you know serious division has arisen in the flock, and the enemy is wrecking havoc in the fellowship. I started working through this transition with the Elders almost two years before I actually stepped down.

It is highly unlikely that this would be the same script for someone else's church, but here is how it played out for our church.

Prior to bringing what I believed I was hearing from God to the Elders, I had been seeking God for three years about who was next. I wasn't at all sure about the *when*, but I needed to know the *who*. I considered various ones to be the leading candidate at different times. When I finally felt like I knew who the person was that God had chosen, I began to discuss the possibility of being the next Pastor with this man. The main issue was that he had an outside position to which he felt called by God, and it wasn't realistic for him to do both. I did not push the issue but just sort of let it drop for a few months. He later came to me and said he and his wife believed that God wanted them to lead the church, and he would make other arrangements for the outside situation. At this point I let it wait another five to six months to see if it really stuck. It did.

Then I came and told the Elders who I thought the next Pastor should be. This young man was well known among the Elders. He had been at the church since first coming as a teen over twenty years earlier. He had served in many different areas in the church and was currently both the Youth Pastor and one of the Elders. I asked them to pray about this choice, still without a timeline. Almost all of the Elders were genuinely highly enthusiastic about this choice. Some wanted time to pray, as well they should. We were meeting bimonthly and two months later everyone was solidly on board except for one Elder. We prayed another two months, and then another. Six months after first bringing this to the Elders we voted to name the next Pastor. The vote was unanimous except for the one brother who abstained. He didn't feel that he was ready to vote yes, but he could definitely move forward in unity with the decision.

By now I had a timeline I felt was from the Lord. My birthday is on February 1, and I would turn 70 the next year. I proposed Informing the congregation concerning the transition on the last Sunday of January right before my 70th birthday. The plan was to tell them that I would be on staff for one more year. I would continue full time for the next six months and then I would serve part time the following six months sharing the Senior Pastor duties with the new guy. When I announced that this would be my last year there was some audible protests from the congregation which was admittedly gratifying. What was more gratifying was when I announced who the new Pastor would be. The congregation stood up and cheered. Praise God!

Probably the most gratifying thing of all was the fact that the congregation did not know this was going to happen. For nine months a small group of about twenty leaders had known about this, and it did not *get out*. That is a truly wonderful testimony to this group of leaders. For the next six months I continued to serve as Senior Pastor while the current Youth Pastor prepared someone to take his place. After six months I stepped back to part time while the new Pastor basically took over. I considered my primary job during this six months to be telling people that the new guy was in charge. As he took over the heavy lifting, I also let him know that if there were things he wanted changed that were likely to be controversial, he should let me go ahead and change them before I stepped down. On the last Sunday of January the new Pastor gave me a ridiculously lavish retirement service, and on February 1 I was fully retired from the staff at our church.

Obviously, someone else's situation is liable to be quite different. I am not suggesting that how we did it is the way to do it. I shared our story because I think there are some general items that should apply in virtually any situation. The most notable ones being the need to recognize and train young leaders, the need to help build support for new leaders, and the need for clear effective communication.

There is an interesting bunny trail post script. I didn't realize this until the new Pastor's birthday on August 31, but when I took the church on July 1, 1988 I was exactly 38 years and 5 months old. When I stepped down on January 31st the new Pastor was 38 years and 5 months old. I felt like it was the Lord saying, "Nailed it."

Do I Stay Or Go?

Once the transition takes place, the question may arise about whether the former Pastor should stay or go. Often this issue is already resolved. In cases where retirement is not involved, the former Pastor is likely to be moving to another church. In cases of retirement, many particular groups have official policies regarding such situations. Usually the former Pastor does not stay. The former Pastor's presence can be a distraction making it difficult for the new leadership; however, this does not have to be the case.

When I came to our church in Smyrna, I took over from my dad. He had been at the church for twelve years and had taken the congregation from under twenty in a tiny rented space to over a hundred in a much better location which they owned (with a mortgage). I actually did not want to come and take this church. We were just coming back from three years in Zimbabwe, and my plan had been to start a new church in a town about forty minutes away. That was *my* plan, but God made it clear that *His* plan was for us to come to Smyrna. It is never a good idea to put your plan ahead of God's plan.

Part of the reason I didn't want to come and take the church at Smyrna was because I knew how the church had been led by my dad. I knew the style of worship and the kind of ideas that guided the church. These things were not wrong or bad, but they were not how I envisioned leading the church. I honestly could not imagine the people attending my dad's church wanting to attend a church under my leadership. Nevertheless, when God directs it is always best to follow.

I was right, and I was wrong. The people at the church were kind to me, but within the first three years at least 75% of the congregation left as new people came in. The Lord was faithful and sent the people we needed. My dad had never really been a part of a church that did things the way I was leading. He was born in 1916 and was more of an Old Time Religion sing-out-of-the-hymnals King James Bible guy. I am sure I made decisions that did not sit well with him; however, he was wonderful. If he had an issue with what I was doing he brought it directly to me and not anyone else. Surprisingly, that was an infrequent event. He supported me among the older folks who stayed, and to the newcomers he and my mom became grandma and grandpa to virtually everyone. My mom passed sixteen years after I came to the church, and my dad passed four years later. Those twenty years were wonderful years that I would not trade for anything.

It may well be that the former Pastor will and should leave the church when the new Pastor comes. But if it is a situation where the former Pastor can stay, the results can be both beneficial and gratifying. The main concern is if the former Pastor is truly willing to step aside. If he or she is unwilling to embrace change and fully endorse the new leadership then they should by all means leave and go elsewhere. But if they will truly step aside and be supportive of the new leadership, they can be of great value to the future of the fellowship.

BITS AND PIECES

Here are a few stories and bits that have been meaningful and helpful to me in my years as a Pastor. Individually none seemed to rate a full chapter, yet, they have been valuable enough to me to insist on being included somewhere. Some are stories, some are lessons learned, and some are simply opinions I have arrived at over the years. Take what is valuable for you and leave the rest.

Where Is Your Office?

I did not myself keep regular office hours nor did I require my Pastoral staff to keep such hours. There were two reasons for this. The first was because being a Pastor is somewhat like being a public school teacher. Teachers have hours they need to be in school. Most people look at those hours and the breaks in the schedule and think that teachers have a pretty cushy situation. They do not see the hours upon hours of work required to be ready to teach while at school, nor the time spent grading papers, meeting with parents, doing continuing education, attending ballgames and events, and on and on. If Pastors are required to clock in their forty hours in the office, they will not survive long, because most of the job takes place outside the office.

The second reason was that the people don't live and work in our office. The *ministry* is not at all limited to services times and scheduled in office meetings. The people are *out there*. They are at their jobs where they can often be visited or taken to lunch. They are shut in at their homes where they need someone to dispel the loneliness. They are at the ballpark or the swim meet, or the recital where they would be honored to see their Pastor attend to watch their kids and grandkids with them.

One of my favorite poems is one I first heard read in my child-hood. It is called *The Preacher's Mistake,* and it is credited to William Croswell Doane, an Episcopal Bishop from 1869 till his death in 1913. Here it is for your edification.

The parish priest
Of austerity,
Climbed up in a high church steeple
To be nearer God
So that he might hand
His word down to His people.
When the sun was high
When the sun was low,
The good man sat unheeding
Sublunary things,
From transcendency
Was he forever reading
And now and again
When he heard the creak
Of the weathervane a-turning
He closed his eyes
And said, "Of a truth
From God I now am learning."
And in sermon script
He daily wrote
What he thought was sent from heaven,
And he dropped this down

On people's heads
Two times one day in seven.
In his age God said,
"Come down and die!"
And he cried out from the steeple,
"Where art thou, Lord?"
And the Lord replied
"Down here among my people."

Retreat or Advance?

This is a silly thing to be sure, but I just want to say something about the asinine notion that when we lead get-aways we should not have *retreats* but only *advances*. This is surely born out of our macho American notion that the Church is some kind of conquering army. This is not an image found in Scripture. We are seen following Christ at His return, but the fighting in this image is done by Him and His Word. When we use this imagery to do worldly endeavors we end up with complete disasters like the Crusades.

We *retreat* in order to get away from all the noise and distractions so we can actually hear more clearly from God. Jesus did this often, and the Bible actually instructs us to do it as well.

Most get-away *advances* involve more noise and distractions with not all that much God. They often pretend to hear from God while laying out visions that are highly non-biblical. Flesh can only give birth to flesh.

Iverna's Story

Iverna Tompkins is one of my favorite preachers. She grew up as a PK and a Pastor's granddaughter. She has taught and Pastored extensively for over forty-five years. One of my favorite stories was one I heard her share that involved her time as a Pastor dealing with a difficult church member.

Iverna was sitting on the platform during a service when she felt the Lord pointing out this particular lady to her. This lady was very difficult to deal with and just generally a pain. To put it bluntly, Iverna didn't like her and neither did hardly anyone else. Iverna felt the Lord say, "Do you see that lady sitting there?"

Iverna replied, "Yes, Lord, I see her."

The Lord said, "I need to discipline her."

Iverna replied, "Yes, Lord, amen. I totally agree."

The Lord said, "I need to discipline her, but I can't."

Iverna asked, "Why are you not able to discipline her, Lord?"

The Lord replied, "I sent her to you and this church so that you would support her and lift her up while I disciplined her, but since she has been with you I've had to support her and lift her up Myself because you won't."

Ouch! We are not called to discipline others. I know there are some rare situations in the New Testament where discipline is necessary, but they are the exception rather than the rule. Some Pastors seem to believe they have a special calling to administer discipline. That is not one of the spiritual gifts. When we discipline in the flesh, the only results can be hurtful. God is well able to discipline His children. When He disciplines positive change happens, but His discipline can be heavy. We are called to bear one another's burdens.

2 Corinthians 7:10 (NIV) *Godly sorrow brings repentance that leads to salvation and leaves no regret, but worldly sorrow brings death.*

God Did Not Abandon Jesus On The Cross.

Jesus cried out from the cross, "My God, my God, why have you forsaken me?" This has led to the foolish notion that God abandoned, or at least turned His face away from, Jesus when He was hanging on the cross. This idea is preached in sermons and promoted in songs to emphasize how dreadful the cross was; however, it is both dangerous and wrong.

This teaching is dangerous because the idea that God turned away from Jesus in His hour of greatest need inevitably leads to the conclusion that He may turn away from us in our hour of greatest need. This idea suggests that He is God of the mountains but not God of the valleys. When things get really tough God will not be there. I am sure that everyone who has ever taught this or sung this would disavow any notion that God would ever leave us, but they are actually saying that this is what God did to Jesus.

I've heard it taught that God turned His face away from Jesus when "He who knew no sin became sin for us," because God was not able to look on sin. Rubbish. If God could not look on sin He could never look at us at all. God looks on sin every minute of every day, and He has for thousands of years.

This teaching is wrong because it is wrong. Jesus was quoting Psalm 22 when He cried out those words. Psalm 22 is clearly the situation of one in great distress. Several of the verses of this Psalm relate directly to what Jesus was experiencing on the cross. The first twenty-one verses are not fun to read, but the Psalm actually has thirty-one verses. The last ten verses seem to be a complete turn around from the first twenty-one. Verse twenty-four actually says:

For he has not despised or scorned
the suffering of the afflicted one;
he has not hidden his face from him
but has listened to his cry for help. Psalms 22:24 (NIV)

So, why did Jesus say this? Why did He utter the anguished cry, "Where are you, God?" I believe the answer lies in Hebrews 4:15: *For we do not have a high priest who is unable to empathize with our weaknesses, but we have one who has been tempted in every way, just as we are—yet he did not sin.* (NIV)

Jesus felt as if God had abandoned Him just as at times we feel as if God has abandoned us. He was tempted in every way that we are tempted, and one of the ways we are tempted is to doubt that God is with us and that He cares.

The truth is that no matter how terrible the situation God has not despised or ignored our suffering. He has not hidden His face from us. He has heard our cry for help. The end result will be Psalm 22:31:

They will proclaim his righteousness,
declaring to a people yet unborn:
He has done it! (NIV)

When The Enemies Of Israel Were Dedicated To Destruction.

One cannot help but have pause at the many times in the story of Israel when God told them to commit genocide and wipe out entire groups of people including children and babies. If that doesn't bother you then, in my humble opinion, there is something wrong with you. I know the Amalekites waylaid Israel when they came up from Egypt, but most of those Saul was sent to kill were not even born at the time. I do not find it at all satisfying to just say, "They deserved it." I personally can simply say that I trust God. I don't have to understand to trust Him.

Nevertheless, I do have a theory to present regarding such situations where God seems to be ruthless and spiteful; killing a fly with a shotgun. What happens to something that is dedicated to Lord, or dedicated to destruction? That which is dedicated to the Lord becomes a sacrifice to Him which means that it becomes holy. Literally these people dedicated to destruction became holy to the Lord.

What does that mean in terms of eternity? Can that which is holy to the Lord also be damned for eternity or does it dwell with the Lord? If you read that suggestion and think that it is crazy talk I can't blame you. The truth is that we don't know how things work on the other side. We don't really have a frame of reference for eternity. We don't have to explain God, and that is a good thing because we can't possibly explain Him. His ways are not our ways. His thoughts are not our thoughts. I'm not offering this suggestion to make us all feel better, though I must admit that it makes me feel better. Regardless of how I may feel I do trust God to always do what it right, and that is enough for me.

Beware Those Who Have The Answers

Three of the most important words you will ever say as a Pastor are, "I don't know." The reason you must learn to say these words is because frequently you don't know. In the natural world "I don't know" can lead to great discoveries, but the natural world is only a tiny fraction of all that really exist. If God is small enough for you, or anyone else, to be able to explain everything He does then He is not the eternal immortal invisible Lord God Almighty.

Occasionally you will encounter someone who seems to have all of the answers. Usually this person will be extremely confident. They will speak with authority and be charismatic. They will likely have a speciality: i.e. End Times, Deliverance, Faith, Hebrew Studies (Tabernacle, Feasts, etc.), the Prophetic, and so forth. Usually these guys (or gals) are bad news coming. Unless their teaching is seasoned with a good deal of humility you need to stay as far away as possible and not endorse them.

At first many of these know-it-alls can seem to be a blessing. You need help, and here is someone who can teach. They will help bring new people into the church. They may even tithe, though that is usually not the case because they have had some revelation or figured out some reason why they are not supposed to tithe. The end result is often at best some confused people when the guru finally leaves, and leave they will. Usually the result is a number of people leaving with them and a significant amount of shipwrecked people no longer in the Faith. At worst they will destroy the church and have zero regret in doing so because, of course, it was someone else's fault and never theirs.

Also, when someone comes in and informs you that they are a prophet, all kinds of alarm bells should go off and red flags start waving. If someone has to tell you they are a prophet they almost certainly are not. They think they are because someone told them they were, or they went to some kind of school to *learn* to be a prophet. If there is actually a prophet in your midst let the Holy Spirit tell you, not some mere person; also, they will not be flashing their Prophet merit badge and assuming authority.

"God Told Me."

The third commandment says that we are not to take the Name of the Lord our God in vain. I was brought up believing that this meant we were not supposed to cuss. I'm not saying that cussing is OK, though I do have to smile every time I see the quote, "I love Jesus but I cuss a little." It is not a good idea to attach any reference to the Lord to any profanity, but taking the name of the Lord in vain is actually something more serious.

I have a friend that I have known since college days who doesn't claim to be a believer. We play golf together often, and the golf course can sometimes give rise to frustrations that may lead to some colorful language. One day one of the fellows playing with us said the words, "God damn." This is pretty much the height of profanity to most American Christians. When this other guy let loose with his GD my friend told me that he really tried to clean up his language around me and that he especially did not use that phrase. I told him, "I can't say those words never escape my lips, but the difference between you and me is that if I do say it I mean it." It isn't often but occasionally my Sons of Thunder side comes to the surface. If you mean it I can't really say that you have taken the Lord's name in vain.

To me taking the Lord's name in vain is attaching His name to something you don't really mean. Christians do this with shocking regularity. I'm not talking about saying "GD." Most Christians avoid that well enough. I am talking about attaching a "Thus saith the Lord" to something that is simply their own idea. Often times it will have to do with what they think they, or you, should do about a certain thing.

It is a wonderful and precious thing to have a real Word from the Lord. It is far more valuable than gold. However, if you are going to say that this is something the Lord has told you then you had better be ready to follow through; otherwise, you have taken the Name of the Lord in vain.

In our church I made it clear that when someone says, "The Lord told me…" that is the end of any conversation about whether or not this is a good idea or the right path. I may not agree with what you say the Lord told you, but if you really believe that the Lord has told you then you have to follow it. The nature of the conversation may shift. "Are you sure the Lord told you?" "I can't go there with you." "How can I help you go there?" But the conversation can no longer be about whether or not this is a good idea or the right path for them to follow.

I think God is less bothered by an unfortunately casual use of His name that someone utters in a moment of stress and frustration than He is by people intentionally attaching His name to their own ideas in order to give them the appearance of being from Him. Thou shalt not take the name of the Lord thy God in vain.

"You Have Bad Spirit!"

When we were a few weeks away from leaving the Bible School in Zimbabwe there was another American missionary who was preparing to come and take our place at the school. This man and his family were making extensive plans to come, but Ezekiel Guti, the man who was over the school, was not yet making any moves to accommodate their coming. This was especially concerning regarding the need for work permits to enter the country. The time was growing short, and I felt compelled to go and speak to him about the need to get busy.

We met and after the necessary greetings and exchange of information about our families I basically opened up with a broadside about how unfair it was for this man to be making such plans while nothing was being done to prepare on this side. I got about two minutes into my complaint when I was brought up short by Ezekiel with the exclamation, "You have bad spirit!" I knew immediately that He was right. I had let myself get so worked up about the situation that while what I was saying may have had merit, that was overshadowed by the wrong spirit I was bringing.

Simply put, being right is not really the most important thing. Being in the right spirit is what really carries weight with God.

The Most Memorable Sermon I Ever Heard.

The greatest sermon I have ever heard was delivered by one of the weakest speakers I have ever heard. The school in Zimbabwe would have an annual Deeper Life Conference. The conference would go for two weeks, and each day would usually involve sermons from just after breakfast until near midnight. There would be many speakers but the main speakers were usually two or three speakers from overseas who would speak multiple times each day.

One year we had a Pastor from Colorado who not only spoke several times each day but who also preached with a lot of gusto and fervor. By the start of the second week he was clearly losing his voice. This Pastor had brought a church member with him who was an accountant. This fellow was in almost every respect what you envision an accountant to be. He was of slight build, balding, middle aged, soft spoken, and retiring. One day at lunch Ezekiel pointed to this accountant and said, "You will be preaching after lunch." I was close to being dumbfounded. Not only was their nothing to suggest that this man was at all a public speaker, but right after lunch was the absolute worst assignment one could draw. It was the middle of summer in Zimbabwe, and the building was not air conditioned. Ushers would patrol the aisles after lunch to poke awake those who had fallen asleep.

The man got up to speak, and within the first two minutes my worst fears were confirmed. The man spoke in an unimpressive monotone. He was virtually motionless and expressionless behind the pulpit. He spoke about Mary and Martha at the occasion of the death of Lazarus. His insight was average at best. It seemed that the ushers had their work cut out for them that afternoon. Then about fifteen or twenty minutes into the sermon something happened.

It is hard to explain exactly what it was that changed. The speaker's voice and body did not change. The temperature in the room did not change. There was no striking revelation from Scripture. The only thing I can say is that we were visited by the Holy Spirit. Though there was nothing visible to the physical eye, it was as if something just poured out over the speaker and then shot out into the room. Within seconds people were running to the front to kneel and pray. The sounds of brokenness and crying were everywhere. The room just fell apart under the weight of the glory and presence of God.

This was a literal demonstration of the bottom line biblical truth expressed so often in Scripture. "Flesh gives birth to flesh. Spirit gives birth to spirit." "Apart from me you can do nothing." "Not by might, nor by power, but by my Spirit says the Lord Almighty." We can study. We can train. We can plan. We can do our best and use our best gifts. But in the end the thing that really matters is the presence and power of God.

The Conclusion of the Matter

Is it worth it?

First of all, in the scope of eternity it is foolish to ask if it is worth it to obey the Lord's call. You simply cannot judge the true outcome of a matter in our limited reference of time and space. Things that may seem to be a waste, or even an abject failure, may in fact be worthwhile and victorious once all of the facts play out and are accounted for.

Back in the late 1970s my wife and I found ourselves with an extra $300. I don't really remember how we came by this extra money, but I do remember that we decided we were supposed to give it away to someone in need. We talked about it and decided to give it to this recently married young couple. Recently married young couples always need money, don't they? We got three crisp one-hundred-dollar bills and put them in an envelope which we left just inside the door to this couple's apartment. Mission accomplished. Thank you Jesus!

Later that week we were in a group with this couple, and they shared about someone giving them $300. We were expecting to hear about how timely this was and that it was an answer to prayer. Instead we heard them say, "We don't know what to do with it."

Did we miss it? Probably. It certainly looked like we simply acted out of our own flesh instead of actually doing something God wanted us to do. However, the story isn't over yet. I don't have a killer follow up about how this did in fact meet a great need. What I do have is enough experience in walking with the Lord to understand that the real answer can only be found in eternity. God plays the long game with us. Perhaps this young couple did have an unexpected need come up? Perhaps they became aware of another need that we would never have known about, and by giving the money to them it ended up being used as God intended? Perhaps this young couple got to experience the joy of giving that led to a lifetime of faithful blessed giving? Perhaps we simply did in fact *miss it*. What I do know it that we learned to be more conscious of being led by God instead of simply acting on our own good ideas.

If one asks whether being a Pastor is worth it, I can respond with great assurance that anytime we obey the Lord it is worth it regardless of what things may look like in the short term. If God has called you and you respond to that call you can be sure that you will receive a reward that far outweighs anything to the contrary in this life.

As someone who has spent thirty-nine years in full time ministry, I can testify that the rewards in this life are also of great worth. Yes, there have been sacrifices, but none that I wouldn't do a hundred times over again. Yes, there have been frustrations, disappointments, and even some heart break, but the Lord has comforted and sustained through them all. But there is more.

As a Pastor you are invited into the most important and life altering events of people's lives. This isn't always fun, but it is always important. If you want to live a life of meaning and significance, you can't do much better, and sometimes it actually is fun. There are the big moments: births, baptisms, marriages, and funerals. There are the ongoing times of walking with people through sickness, family crises, and times of want, waiting, and uncertainty. There are the times of repentance and reconciliation which are usually my favorite times. There is the great privilege of getting to mentor and disciple those who are genuinely serious about following the Lord.

If you are privileged to be able to serve a local church for a long period the blessings can multiply. You dedicate babies for young couples, and then before you know it you are dedicating those babies' babies. You get to truly enter into the story of people's lives. There is the widow or widower you attended in their grief as you presided over the burial of their loved one, and then you see them slowly return from the darkness of their grief and perhaps even have the joy of seeing them find a new life partner. There are the parents with whom you share their burden for a prodigal son or daughter, and with whom you rejoice when the prodigal returns and experiences the great joy of coming back to the Father. After Pastoring the same local church for thirty-three years I know first hand the stories, and the stories behind the stories, of God's wonderful grace and power.

One of my favorite things about being a Pastor is to simply look out over the congregation during a worship service. I see people whose lives have been dealt a severe blow with their hands raised and tears on their faces giving a true sacrifice of praise to God. I see others starting to grow in faithfulness and beginning to experience the freedom that comes as they start to trust the presence of the Lord. Yes, I also see empty seats and missing persons. There is heartbreak, but this is also a time when the Lord speaks quite clearly to His servant. This is the under-shepherd taking stock of the flock which has been entrusted to his care. As the under-shepherd takes stock, the Great Shepherd speaks, and what a wonderful terrible remarkable privilege it is to hear Him.

Is it worth it? I believe it is worth it in this life. There are struggles and challenges to be sure, but any life of meaning will contain those. I know it is worth it in the life to come because God's Word assures us of this. To those called to shepherd God's flock, and who faithfully serve Peter writes: "And when the Chief Shepherd appears, you will receive the crown of glory that will never fade away." Peter 5:4 (NIV)

Also Available From

WORDCRAFTS PRESS

In the Boat with Jesus
Marian Rizzo

Illuminations
Paula K. Parker & Tracy H. Sugg

Questing
Wayne Berry

Devotions from the Barn Door
Tammy Chandler

Morning Mist
Barbie Loflin

www.wordcrafts.net

www.ingramcontent.com/pod-product-compliance
Lightning Source LLC
Chambersburg PA
CBHW031421120626
46545CB00006B/2214